THE ALL NEW GOD, SEX AND MONEY DIET

THE ALL NEW GOD, SEX AND MONEY DIET

BOOK 1: THE BEGINNING

TRUDY WAKEFIELD

Copyright © 2023 Trudy Wakefield All rights reserved

This work depicts actual events in the life of the author as truthfully as recollection permits and/or can be verified by research. Occasionally, dialogue consistent with the character or nature of the person speaking has been supplemented. All persons within are actual individuals; there are no composite characters. The names of some people have been changed to maintain their privacy.

No part of this book may be reproduced, or stored in a retrieval system, or transmitted in any form or by any means, electronic, mechanical, photocopying, recording, or otherwise, without express written permission of the publisher.

ISBN-13: 979-8-9884668-0-2

Cover design by: The Bloom, LLC
Library of Congress Control Number: 2018675309
Printed in the United States of America

Published by The Bloom Press

For my children

Emma
Rees
Clare

And anyone else who has thought of me as Mom

CHAPTER I

IN WHICH
Your Mother Achieves Terminal Velocity in a Suzuki Samurai

1.1

So I married a narcissist, kids. In my defense, I didn't know your father was a douchebag. How could I recognize a narcissist when I was surrounded by narcissists from birth? In your father's defense, he didn't know he was a narcissist, either. But then again, to be a narcissist, you can never admit that you are one.

Can a narcissist ever change? From all I've read, the answer is no. A narcissist can't change. But then again, I believe an alcoholic can stop drinking and a drug addict can stop taking drugs. So I look at narcissism in the same way. First off, the narcissist has to admit they have a problem, just like any addict would have to do. From there, I believe anything is possible; just ask a recovering alcoholic. That being said, I do not know very many recovering narcissists. This explanation might help you kids understand some of the messed-up years you were thrown into the moment you were born. But don't worry; this is only the middle of my story, not the end. So hang in there and have hope.

It all began the moment your dad and I said, "I do." A counselor would later tell us that we became family the instant we got married. And that's all fine and good when both marriage partners come from a healthy family, but not so good in our case. I'm not a psychologist or psychiatrist, but I'm certain no one is born a narcissist, just like no one is born an enabler. We were products of our childhood. So to say we didn't come from healthy homes is evident.

In addition, your dad and I were never meant to be together. David lived in a beautiful home on a lake outside of Olympia, Washington. I lived an hour-and-a-half away in a half-finished house down a long, nasty dirt road. David's family had money; his father was the vice president of sales for an industrial company, and his mother ran a Christian bookstore they owned.

Even though my father had managed to go to college and become part owner of a physical therapy business, my family always struggled financially and for generations had lived in poverty. David lived a socially cultured life filled with European trips and vacation homes. Our "culture" consisted of gardening, church, and visiting extended family. And church was the real difference: I was Seventh-day Adventist. David was Baptist. Those groups mix about as well as Adventists and Catholics, or Adventists and Presbyterians, or Adventists and anyone other than Adventists. Although they all believe that there was a guy named Jesus, that's as far as it gets. Even so, fate somehow conspired for David and me to stumble into each other at a high school halfway between the eighty miles that separated us.

But before I go too far ahead, kids, let me make it completely clear how different Adventists' beliefs are than other Christians and quite a bit different than the rest of humanity. Seventh-day Adventists tend to separate themselves from the masses. They stick with their own. They go to church on Saturday and believe that going to church on Sunday is a sin. They don't wear jewelry, smoke, drink alcohol or caffeine, eat meat, play cards other than Rook, or consort with sinners who do those things unless they have to. They believe they have a special revelation given to them by their prophet Ellen G. White: The Three Angels Message. With all the widespread apostasy in the world, it is the responsibility of the Remnant (that's Adventists) to warn the apostates (that's everyone else) of their sin and prepare them for the imminent return of Jesus. Of course, this means that only they will go to Heaven. All things considered, it makes sense for Adventist parents to send their kids to Adventist schools to protect them from the evils of the world.

My family and siblings were no exception to the norm. Like my brother and sister before me, I went to an Adventist boarding school for high school. The twelve-hour school days, combined with a nocturnal roommate, proved too much for me. Just after the holidays in my freshman year, I had a nervous breakdown. I moved out of the dorm and finished the spring term with a family off-campus. I hadn't recovered enough to go back my sophomore year, so my parents found a Baptist high school forty-five minutes away that I could attend for the interim. But as you can imagine, they had significant concerns about what kinds of influences might come my way should I attend a school outside my faith. I was sixteen, sheltered from the world outside of Adventism, and scared of losing my faith among all the non-remnant Christians. Who knows what would happen if I became, God forbid, a Baptist.

Every fall, the school year started with a picnic and social event at a nearby park. It was a chance for all hundred and fifty high school kids to have fun, socialize, and get to know the new students. A kind new friend took the time to introduce me to my classmates. She knew everyone because she was one of those students who had attended Tacoma Baptist since kindergarten. Considering that the sophomore class had only forty-two students, it was not an unrealistic or extremely time-consuming task for me to meet everyone.

"Now I want you to meet David," she told me as we walked away from a knot of girls and towards another group of people.

"Thank you," I replied, not sure what to expect next.

"He's got arthritis. He's such a great testimony for the Lord."

1.2

Okay, kids, you're going to have to bear with me through all the Jesus language. I can't tell you the story any other way because it's how I thought and spoke back then. And please know I was quite sincere. Granted, my motivation was not to go to hell, but we'll talk more about that later. So back to the story.

1.3

"He's such a great testimony for the Lord," my friend said.

And so it was that I saw David for the first time. He was my height, lean, and pleasing to look at, although he did have a Mr. Roger's haircut. It also struck me as odd that he was wearing a brown, button-up shirt tucked into dress slacks and Birkenstocks on his socked feet. Everyone else had on jeans, a T-shirt, and tennis shoes. The school's restrictive dress code had been relaxed because it was a social event, and everyone–except David, that is–jumped at an opportunity to dress down. I watched him chat with a few classmates and could see he was trying hard to please everyone. He seemed to enjoy the attention and did manage the largish group quite well.

It also occurred to me that he had an agenda. *Hmm*, I thought. *What's his angle?* I could tell he was popular, but it certainly wasn't because he was a jock. His clothes and lean build proved that not to be the case. He definitely wasn't a bad boy or the class clown. Then it finally dawned on me: *He's not into sports; he's into politics!* I smiled knowingly.

"David," said my friend, "I'd like you to meet Trudy. She's new and in our class." His attention turned away from the group he was working and towards me as I extended my hand. He smiled and shook it politely.

"Hello," he began, easing into greeting mode.

"You must be our class president," I replied.

David stopped shaking my hand but didn't let go. For just a moment, his brow furrowed, his large cow-brown eyes looked questioningly into mine, and he was speechless. I had stunned him. For so much talk and apparent self-confidence, he faltered, finding it a surprise to already be known by a complete stranger. I had called it! I knew exactly who and what he was. I was not at all overawed by him, even though I felt I was supposed to be. His shocked eyes looked kind, despite his somewhat obvious self-involved behavior. He was well-groomed and obviously had never known need. He oozed wealth that few in our little school had.

His over-compensating confidence was for political reasons; that was true. But he also had a compelling presence. At the tender age of sixteen, his eyebrows and face already told a story as they wrinkled inquisitively towards me. More importantly, he showed confidence in his own skin and seemed unconcerned that his appearance stood out and that he was most obviously the rich kid in the school. Let's just say that he was compelling, but not in the way he desired to be. I wanted to know him better.

He resumed shaking my hand as he regained composure. Then he stiffly leaned inward toward me, another political move to show me his warmest regard. "Trudy, is it?" he asked, adding a rather large artificial smile.

"Yes, it is."

"Well, yes, I am the class president," he said with slight bewilderment in his voice.

"Ah, I thought so."

"Welcome to TBS," he said politely and kindly, finally back in his comfort zone. Then he turned to resume his previous banter and jokes with our classmates, not wanting to waste his agenda at hand. And it was my turn to leave that group to be introduced to even more new faces.

At home later that evening, my mom asked if I had met any boys that interested me. With a twinkle in her eye, she turned on the television.

"There's two guys," I replied. Since I'd met most of the high school in a single day, I was able to sort out my options pretty quickly. "I like James," I said wistfully. "He plays football but seems like a really nice guy, too. And there might be one other guy I'm curious to know better. His name is David. He'

"Oh?" came my mother's response as the twinkle in her eyes grew, wanting to get the dirt.

"Yeah. Well, we'll see." I cut the subject short and allowed the television to fill in the silence.

1.4

My sophomore school year went on and proved to be one of the happiest years ever. I joined the band and got a new set of friends. I found a boyfriend. Surprisingly, I never did have any classes with David that year. So my curiosity about him eventually went by the wayside. I did know he was the smartest student in my class. I knew he missed a lot of school for doctor's appointments and was frequently sick. I knew arthritis kept him from playing baseball like he had his freshman year and that the coach cut him from the team. But he, like my sophomore year, slowly drifted by.

Another short Washington summer came and went before the school year began once again. My parents had seen how well I did at Tacoma Baptist and very cautiously permitted me to attend another year. Even though I was excited to be there, things were not going so well with my boyfriend. He was nice and all; I just knew I would never be in love with him. I also didn't know what to say or how to end the relationship. Perhaps there were signs all along. Like every other non-Adventist, he complained about our food. Of course, I grew up a strict Seventh-day Adventist vegetarian.

Now, I've had good vegetarian food, and it's nothing like Adventist food. It's amazing what modern-day technology can do with soy. With enough processing, flavoring, and coloring, Adventists have managed to turn the humble soybean into all kinds of meats. Incredibly, they had soy ham, soy turkey, soy chicken, soy hot dogs, soy bacon, soy sausage, soy lunch meat, and even soy tuna. You name it—you could buy it in a can with a label that roughly approximated what meat the soy was supposed to be. In our pantry, we had cans of Skallops, Tuno, FriChick, and the perpetually confusing Nuteena, which, no matter what was done with it, always ended up with the appearance and odor of canned dog food mixed in peanut butter.

Now having eaten both real and fake meat, there is no comparison between soy chicken and real chicken. It would be like the moon trying to be the sun or a car tire trying to be a steak. It just isn't possible. However, having eaten these foods all of my life, I found it quite rude when my Baptist boyfriend complained about a Turkee sandwich.

He also couldn't stand the road I lived on. We called it the power line road, but it was barely a road at all. You had to drive a mile and a half on what used to be gravel with potholes so large they swallowed small cars on rainy days. No joke. It happened. But the last thing I wanted was to hear my boyfriend complain about my family's food and that our road was going to get his car dirty. After six months of dealing with his gripes, I had decided that whoever I married would never, ever, complain about my family's food, our road, or our

11

Seventh-day Adventist beliefs. I truly meant it, too. But that didn't solve the dilemma of how to break up with Robert. Somehow, "You don't like the road I live on or Prosage Patties" didn't seem like a good enough explanation.

September was drawing to a close, bringing with it shorter days and more rain. In my junior year, I had several classes with David. One day in Bible class, my neighbor plopped a small note on my desk, TRUDY written on it in unfamiliar handwriting. Inside it said, "Hey, just as friends, I was wondering if you wanted to go to Point Defiance with me? –David."

Bible class was profoundly dull. Mr. Bucket spent the entire period sitting in a chair next to the overhead projector, writing on a transparency. That year we studied the Pentateuch, the first five books of the Bible. We had made it to Exodus.

"Chapter 25," Mr. Bucket blathered on, putting a new transparency on the projector. "In chapter 25, we learn about how God commanded Moses to build the ark of the covenant and the tabernacle." He wrote down "CH 25: Instructions for Ark of the Covenant and Tabernacle" on the overhead. The students who weren't passing notes to their friends or asleep copied what he wrote.

"Now the ark was to be made of shittim wood." A snicker came from the back corner of the room. Mr. Bucket looked up, and everyone appeared to pay attention. Then he looked down, and things went back to normal. Another note addressed to someone else landed on my desk, pausing on its way across the classroom. "Now shittim. . ." another snicker. He looked up again, and I held the note for a second, waiting until he went back to writing before passing it across the aisle. "Shittim is what we would call the acacia tree." He wrote "shittim = acacia tree" on the transparency. "Okay," he continued, turning a page in his Bible. "Now for chapter 26. Chapter 26 is about the curtains of the Tabernacle." I quickly looked back at David's note. He seemed like a nice guy. "Sure!" I jotted on the paper, folded it back up, and handed it across the aisle. Our first date was set.

1.5

It was a beautiful first day of October. Not a cloud blotted the sky when school finally ended, and I climbed into David's red Suzuki Samurai. As I closed the door, I heard the metal clink hollowly. The small boxy car felt and looked a lot like a tinker toy. I had never been in such a tiny car before, but I could see how it could be useful. It went anywhere, loved to get dirty, and could easily fit in a large enough pocket. Before I knew it, we were off. It was a little strange to be sitting next to a sixteen-year-old who wore dress slacks with Birkenstocks, looked and acted somewhat like a profoundly self-absorbed Fred Rogers, and drove a tiny little car. Strangely, it somehow fit, and I relaxed a little more in my short seat. *We're just friends, it's not a date, we're just friends,* I sighed to myself.

We had just merged onto I-5 when David hit me with his first question. "What do you think about the laws of man, Trudy?" It caught me a bit off guard, and he let it hang in the air.

"What kind of laws are you talking about?" I replied, not knowing where he was trying to lead me.

"Well, the laws our government has instated and the general laws that we follow as a society," he replied smugly. He was up to something. *Ahh, he's fishing to see how holy I am*, I thought. *Well, two can play at this game.*

"I think we should keep them because Jesus kept the laws of his time," I replied. I took the safe road. No Christian could argue what Jesus did, and it affirmed my holiness. A self-righteous smile spread over his face. I seemed to have confirmed his internal dialogue.

"That is why I only drive 55 miles per hour. I Peter 2:13 says that we need to submit to every ordinance of man for the Lord's sake. *Every* ordinance. The speed limit is a law of man, so I will honor it, and by honoring man's law, I am honoring God."

There, he said it. Unlike all his other young classmates enjoying the freedom of driving with the speed of traffic and God forbid even in the left lane, David chose holiness over hell. This also explained why every other vehicle on the interstate kept passing us, including fully loaded semis and what appeared to be someone's great-grandmother. Indeed, he truly was holy, because I saw that he had even set his cruise control to 55 to ensure he would not sin by breaking man's law. Deep down inside, I knew that no matter how holy I wanted to be, when I got my license, I would probably still speed. Yet, of the two people in the baby Jeep that day, one of us seemed to be missing a larger point in life's lessons. This thought continued in my mind as another semi passed us, blowing us sideways and reminding me that his vehicle had zero noise insulation.

Finally, our longer-than-normal drive ended as we entered Point Defiance Park. It was a lovely afternoon, one of the last pleasant days of fall before the rains set in and the sun disappears until next July. The flower gardens had finished blooming, but the maples were in full color, orange-red against the azure sky. I was more comfortable there than anywhere else he could have taken me. Being outclassed economically, I could let my guard down in a park easier and not have to worry about social expectations. My family loved being outdoors; it was safe and absolutely predictable. Nature obeyed only nature's laws and removed all social obligations.

The colorful leaves were dry enough to crunch under my feet, an unusual delight. Usually, they were soggy, wet, and stuck to my shoes. The cool, crisp air reminded me that today was meant to be enjoyed. *Tomorrow the rain may come, but today is beautiful,* I thought as we walked through the park. Just as I was beginning to relax, David's caught me off-guard again.

"So, I have a question for you, Trudy."

"Okay?" came my reluctant response. *Is this going to be another "laws of God" thing?* I braced myself.

"What does Susan think of me?" he asked.

What! Today wasn't about me or getting to know me as a

"friend" at all. *He just brought me here to get to my best friend!* A sense of hurt, regret and embarrassment filled me, but I stuffed it away, regaining my composure once again.

"Well, I think she likes you. Definitely as a friend for sure. I don't know if there's more to it or not," came my calm, maybe too calm of a response. It seemed to be good enough as he absorbed my words, finding enough hope in them to continue.

"Well, good! I think I might ask her out then." Our stroll took us up a hill.

"Yeah, I am sure that you will be good for each other. You're both such wonderful people." Now that I realized he didn't want me, I was able to adjust to his new game. And just as suddenly as it began, it ended.

"So, how do you like Tacoma Baptist so far? His next question once again took me off guard. My mind tried to grasp how he could go from using me to set him up with my best friend to what seemed to be a genuine interest in me again. I was befuddled, but kept trying.

"I'm back for a second year, so I guess I like it well enough not to go back to my other school," came my response. I might have overstated the obvious.

"Well, I'm glad your back," he said with a large grin on his face and a chuckle in his voice, knowing that he might have asked a dumb question.

"Me, too," I replied, trying to ease the tension. And from that point on, our time together was quite pleasant. The more we talked, the more I realized that David was self-absorbed, but not an entire asshole. He seemed to have great social skills in a crowd, but one-on-one, he was extremely blunt and had a tendency to say exactly what he thought. Exactly. *Why beat around the bush when we can get down to the real stuff* seemed to be his philosophy. And he did appear to care about me, just not enough to take me behind a tree and make out. Also, one huge advantage of his liking my best friend was that I truly had nothing to prove to him. I could be myself, the self I feared wasn't good enough for a rich, smart kid like David. Before long, the conversation was filled with laughter, jokes, and a sense of true friendship that comes between anyone who has things in common.

"So, is that a birthmark on your neck?" I asked as we wandered around the Japanese garden, looking at all the leftover plants of summer.

"Well, no."

"Really? It looks like one."

"Actually, that's my real skin color. The rest of me is a birthmark. It's just that one spot on my neck that reveals my true skin color."

I never could quite figure out what to expect from him. It's like every time I took a right, he reversed directions, doubled back, and then confused me and made me laugh at the same time. But the best part was this: When I was twelve, I had open heart surgery, and none of my friends comprehended what I went through. But with David, I could talk about my surgery and fear of death freely with someone my own age. Just as my surgery had marked and separated me from my peers, so also had his arthritis. For the first time in either of our lives, we found a friend who had faced hard things and could understand what it meant.

As the autumn sun sunk below the trees, it brought the chill of damp marine air. I put on my jacket. David seemed completely unaffected by the dropping temperature as we slowly wandered back to his lunchbox of a car. Time was up: the date was over and he had to drive me a half hour home and then drive over an hour to his house. The space between us felt warm, inviting and pleasing. It was nice to be near him.

The dinner hour had come and gone. My stomach growled as we made our way out of the park. David didn't seem to notice: I would get no offer of dinner on this date. I was a little surprised and still hungry, but also relieved. I didn't have to worry about embarrassing myself with him in a restaurant because I wasn't culturally as well-trained.

Before long, we got back on the freeway, David owning the right lane with the cruise control set. We chatted throughout the drive, but as we got closer to my home, a new dread began to creep over me. We would have to go down the final road to my house, the miserable power line road that every other guy hated so passionately. I prepared myself for his inevitable comments and complaints.

He turned onto the road, crossed the bridge going over a small creek, and came to a full stop on a rise. I could see him surveying the narrow road, filled with massive potholes and deep ruts. The huge power lines hummed above us. *Oh God, he's not even going to try to drive it,* I thought to myself in horror. *At least all the other dates drove me home!*

"So, this is your road?" he asked curiously.

"Yes, I know, it's a really bad road," came my response as I wanted so desperately to hide and disappear from embarrassment. But before I could, he laughed.

"Are you buckled up?" he asked, looking over at me and assessing my seating. That question took me by complete surprise. *Why does he care?*

He reached over and checked my seat belt. "Pull on the strap to make sure it's tight."

"Okay?" I said while pulling my seat belt tight.

"Now there's a handle to hold on to there," he pointed, "and there."

I reached out and tentatively grabbed the handles.

"Are you ready?"

"Ready for what?" came my response. He didn't answer; he just put his Samurai into first gear and stepped on it. For all the talk about honoring God's and man's laws on pavement, all rules were off when it came to dirt roads. Were there any speed limit signs? Nope, so he could go as fast as he wanted without any nasty issues of conscience. A cloud of rocks and exhaust billowed behind us. I could have sworn he had a rocket strapped to the car.

We nearly levitated down the road. My dad drove the road fast, too fast. But nothing compared to these mind-blowing, screaming come-to-Jesus speeds. We were going about nine thousand miles an hour before we got to the first big pothole. Now, my dad wisely drove around them. Thirty feet long and filled with water, it stood no chance with David. A wall of brown, chunky mud puddle sprayed over the hood and we slowed, but only because of the water and mud. He pushed down on the gas harder and we maintained our supersonic speed out of the puddle and into the air. All four tires spun in the firmament for a half-second before we hit and raced off again. My head smacked against the fabric top.

If, at that moment, I had taken time to think, I would have been grateful that it wasn't a solid top because I hit it again when we cleared the next puddle. As it was, I needed all my concentration not to fall out. I don't know if I ever really sat in the seat. I was too stunned to say anything, but David didn't seem to have that problem. He whooped at every puddle and laughed at each jump. To him, this beat any carnival ride. The Zipper? The Gravitron? Mere child's play compared to flying a small vehicle down my road. No brakes, no turning to avoid things. The shock of it all overwhelmed me as I tried to simultaneously grasp what was happening and somehow keep my head from punching a hole through his roof. And just quickly as it began, it ended.

"Thanks! That was fun!" he exclaimed as he finally pushed on the brakes, and we ever so slowly pulled into my parent's driveway. I was truly speechless. My body and mind had entered shock. I had never, ever been down the power line road at that speed.

David's face was all smiles as he hopped out of the car, lighter and less stiff than before. My father rounded the corner of the house, pushing a wheelbarrow filled with boxwood shrubs as I slowly and reluctantly pulled my shell-shocked body out of the car. First, my toes touched the ground, slowing the vibrations and jolts that seemed to be echoing up and down my spine. The solid ground calmed me, and I reentered reality and proceeded to introduce David to my dad.

"Hey, Dad, this is my friend, David," I said, trying to explain to David in my mind why my father was dressed in a torn t-shirt and stained jeans and planting boxwood. These precious few hours at the end of a work day were my father's therapy. The more worn, torn, and stained his clothes, the happier he was. It wasn't that my father wasn't educated because he was. It's just that he lacked an understanding of social protocols. David, always knowing his obligations, approached my Dad and greeted him, ready to shake his hand. My father missed the cue as he packed dirt around the newly placed shrub.

"So, what are you planting?" David, being quick on his feet, dismissed my father's obvious social breach.

"Boxwood."

"Is that some kind of shrub?" David asked, almost being overly polite.

"Yup," replied my father as he reached for the next plant. A long awkward silence filled the air as I tried to think of anything else to say to help smooth over the two worlds that had just crashed into each other.

"It'll be two to three years, then there'll be a hedge right here," my dad said in a matter-of-fact voice.

"Thank you so much for bringing me home, David," I said, drawing the attention away from my father and his strange social habits. David looked at me, somewhat surprised, yet getting the hint that our date was over and it was time for him to leave now. I wasn't about to let him in our house, still half-finished after fifteen years.

"Not a problem. Thank you for a wonderful time," he

replied ever so politely. "Well, it was very nice to meet you, Mr. Pflugrad," David courteously said as he turned back to his toy car.

"Uh huh," grunted my Dad as he reached for another plant.

David drove off slowly down our long driveway, but I thought I caught a hint of his engine revving as he turned the corner onto the power line road.

I turned to go in the house and made my way down our still-unfinished wooden stairs to the only part of our home that was carpeted and had painted walls. "So, how did it go?" my mother asked with a twinkle in her eyes. *She's just looking for dirt*, I thought. "It was fine," came my reply. My stomach once again reminded me that he didn't offer me dinner. From the looks of it, no one had cooked here, either. I guess I had to figure it out on my own.

"He has a crush on Susan," came my reply as I looked searchingly in the refrigerator for some kind of food to eat. Every shelf was stuffed full of containers filled with leftovers, but from when? The ones in the back were definitely alive and had a vibrant, dynamic social structure, but even the plastic containers in front were unreliable, suspect to the rapidly evolving and apparently malevolent society of the cheese drawer. I would never trust one of those. I shut the refrigerator and began to consider secondary options.

"Oh?" she continued to probe. I wasn't in the mood to talk about it. My mind was confused about the whole thing. *PB and J!* I thought to myself, resolving at least one problem in my mind—as long as the bread hadn't gone moldy.

"Yeah, I'll talk to her about it sometime tomorrow and see what comes of it," came my reply as I started spreading peanut butter on a slice.

"He didn't take you out to dinner?" my mom chirped.

"Nope," was all I could say with a mouth full of stickiness. I really didn't want to talk. My heart pounded and my head spun with curious questions and thoughts. I needed to be alone but not draw a scene. So, I had to wait. I slumped onto the living room loveseat all too close to the raging hot wood stove.

Apparently, I hadn't given my mom enough information. She looked at me expectantly, waiting for more. *I have to appease her, or she won't leave me alone,* I thought to myself.

"We had a very pleasant time. I think we'll be friends. I can't think of two people I admire more and it's fitting that they be together." There, I said it. She got what she was looking for. I plastered a smile on my face and gave her one more morsel of dirt to make sure she wouldn't bug me anymore.

"He likes our dirt road," I said bluntly as I crammed the

last of my sandwich into my mouth. "He likes it a lot." I stared blankly at the T.V. That one statement stopped her probing. She also knew my three requirements for my future husband. *Whooda thought* seemed to be the question that hung in the air. It worked! It shut her up.

Just then, the sliding glass door opened, and my father walked in, dirt covering his hands and clothes. He looked at me curiously for a second and then at my mother, who still was pondering the details of my adventure. He said nothing and walked to his spot on the couch.

"Lester! You better not sit down in your work clothes," she snapped. Without a word, he turned and disappeared down the hall to appease my mother's disapproval.

I quickly acted, seeing my chance to leave and take my thoughts with me. "I have homework to get done before bed," I said as I stood up. Then, as quickly as possible, I made my way up our cold, damp unfinished stairs and down the uncarpeted hallway to my bedroom. I closed the door behind me and leaned on it, sighing heavily.

It's over, I thought to myself as I collapsed onto my bed. I looked out my dark window and into the evening sky. My mind was spinning, but my heart felt a peace I had never known before. It was as if I had come home for the first time. I thought it was strange how I felt more like myself with him than with my current boyfriend. It made me both glad and confused. I had a new friend I could be myself with. And he was intriguing. My thoughts made me curious and stumped me at the same time. *A crippled Mr. Rogers for a husband?* I shrugged it away, rolled over, and closed my eyes.

CHAPTER II

IN WHICH
Your Father Rescues Your Mother From the Girls' Bathroom

2.1

For the next several weeks, David was blissfully happy as our friendship continued to grow. And, to top it off, he had finally captured the woman of his dreams. During his latest trip to Europe with his family, he discovered his perfect type; she had to look European, with dark hair, olive skin and beautiful features. It just turned out that his perfect woman also happened to be my best friend, Susan.

In a short amount of time, I managed to become an advisor and counselor for both David and Susan. David picked my brain to learn everything he could about her while Susan talked to me about the ups and downs of dating David. Eventually, the downs became more prevalent than the ups in their courtship. David one-on-one was much different than David the class president. Sure, David loved to have fun and crack a joke, but when it came to issues of faith and religion, he was entirely serious.

"Why does he always ask what I'm thinking all the time on our dates?" Susan asked over lunch one day, annoyed.

"I don't know," I replied. "Maybe he wants to know what you are thinking at the moment."

"Yeah, but he asks ALL THE TIME," she said in exasperation.

I knew exactly what she was talking about. There couldn't be more than five seconds of quiet in a conversation before David would ask me the same thing. I found it humorous, myself. He was a seeker like me, and always looking for the deeper meaning in life. If you didn't have a thought at the moment, ask what the other person was thinking about, and maybe you could find some answers, was his logic.

But perhaps Susan wasn't always into probing the depths of the universe twenty-four hours a day. Perhaps, in fact, she was simply looking to have a good time and simply accepted life for what it was. Perhaps, she was even looking to have a little fun! David, however, was completely incapable of understanding why anyone would want to live life that way.

"How could anyone go through life and not care?" he asked me one afternoon as we sat on the shores of Wapato Lake, our feet pressing into the damp grass. Over the past month, we had been spending more time together, particularly because I was able to interpret Susan for him. "I mean, doesn't that matter to her?"

"You can't look at it that way, Dave," I said, trapped in a hopeless romantic-comedy love triangle. "Not everyone thinks like you do about things."

"That's stupid," he said with certainty, avoiding ambiguity at all costs. "Did you know that once people turn eighteen to twenty-three, they *never change?*" He said the words in horror as though they were committing the Unpardonable Sin. "It's like they just give up trying to be a better person."

"It's not like that," I tried again. "Some people don't worry about those things. Not everyone feels that every moment of our existence has to be more than it really is."

"But we are commanded to be holy," he retorted, and popped a tiny Bible out of his pocket with print so small that it had a built-in magnifying glass. This is not an exaggeration, kids; I'm being honest; this DID happen. He flipped through the rolling-paper thin pages for a few seconds, then double-checked with the magnifying glass. "Here it is," he triumphed. "Matthew 5:48: 'Be ye therefore perfect, even as your Father which is in heaven is perfect.'" Of course, he quoted from the King James Version, by far the most holy translation. "See? We are told to be perfect, so not following God's commandments is like saying you want to go to hell."

I laughed inadvertently, surprised at his black/white, either/or thinking.

"What?" he said, clueless. "I'm serious." He squinted at his Bible again, trying to find another verse. "And I can prove it."

The All New God, Sex and Money Diet

2.2

The relationship was obviously doomed from the beginning, and within a month, I ended up being there for Susan, who gratefully ended her moody, philosophical dating experience with David. And poor David had his heart broken for the first time in his young years. Never before had he been, should I put it so bluntly, dumped. And who did he turn to? His newest best friend, of course: Me. I spent my days consoling one for doing the right thing and wiping away tears of a broken heart for the other.

There was no texting or email in the mid 90's when your dad and I were in high school. Letters came by paper, written with real ink and graphite. Sometimes I just needed to write something but was stuck in class and didn't want to fight my way through the crowded hallways between classes to find whoever it was to say whatever needed to be said. So, while the lecture droned on, I ripped out a piece of notebook paper, passionately professed my thoughts, folded the paper, wrote the person's name on it, and passed it down the row of desks.

Row by row, hand by hand, these letters repeatedly passed

back and forth between us. Often small notes like "Hi!!!" or a smiley face got scribbled along the way as the note made its way across seven rows of desks. But no one, absolutely no one, would dare to open the sacred note. It was the unspoken trust that our classmates shared with one another. Notes Must Be Passed.

If we didn't have that class together, David and I would still write notes and hand them off in the hallway between classes. And with each note, we grew closer to each other. Yes, kids, we've kept our letters to each other all these years. Yes, we are that sappy. But, it was a rather rough beginning. Think of these notes as texting messages back and forth. And keep in mind how holy we wanted to be. It will reflect in the language of our notes to each other. Don't say I didn't warn you.

To help follow the who's saying what, my writing is italicized.

2.3

How are you doing?

I hurt today, Trudy. I can't look at Susan, let alone think about her. I hate this! I guess I am expecting myself to take this quicker than I am.

I'm really sorry about that. I know it is hard. Realize that it's hard for her too. I know it is because it was hard for me. Still is. I wish that I could say the magic words to make you feel better, but I can't. It's going to take time. You'll get over it. I still feel bad, though. Just keep smiling and know that God has it all in his hands.

This isn't your fault. None of it is. How could you know that she didn't really like me? Please, I beg of you, don't feel bad. As I said on October 1st, just knowing that she had liked me at one time is enough to make me happy. I am happy, but it is kind of an ironic happiness.

David Wakefield, will you stop it! Knock it off! You're going to drive yourself crazy, and all the rest of us included!

2.4

What did you put in your water?

Lemon juice concentrate. I accidentally put a little too much in today.

I like it!

So do I. I drink lemon juice straight from the bottle at home. It's a lot stronger than eating lemons.

I bet! I don't think that I'd like it that much.

I am not quite sure why I do either. Have you asked John to the Tolo yet?

No, I haven't asked anyone.

Do you have a relationship with John?

That's an interesting question. I guess I'm making our relationship into more of a friendship. I'm telling people that things are the same until they are finalized.

I know how that goes. I sure hope it works out for you.

I do too, Dave. If you'd like, you could pray for me. I think we're going to talk during lunch. I don't want anyone to get hurt.

2.5

In addition to being there for my two friends, I knew I had long passed my obligation of finally terminating my own relationship with John. Day after day, I put off the inevitable task that had to be done. But how could I do it and not hurt his feelings? I took the easy way out and handed him a Dear John letter at lunch the next day. So that ended my relationship with him, and I sighed a short breath of relief; I was happy to move on. It was cruel, cowardly, and I hated myself for it, but I was finally free. For better or worse, the deed was done. But I never wanted to ever, ever, do that again. Relationships were hard, and I dreaded being hurt or hurting anyone.

Eventually, David and I developed a true friendship. Soon we spent afternoons after school going to parks, taking walks, and never, ever going out to eat. My grumbling stomach became my constant companion when I was with David. One early spring day at Snake Lake in Tacoma, as the lilies and cattails just had begun to poke out of the marshy water, we started to share out secrets.

"I'm done with women," David said, his eyes on the filmy

water that swirled beneath us. We sat on the edge of the boardwalk, our legs brushing the still young, green cattails. "I can't have a good relationship."

"You know that's not true," I said. "You just haven't found the right person."

"I'm going to become a monk. I've thought it out, and there's a monastery in Oregon that I can go to. They let you try it out for six months. I'm going to devote my life to prayer and self-denial. Perhaps if it is God's will, I will die a martyr."

Oh, how holy can you be? I thought to myself. "Are you sure that would work?" I replied doubtfully. "Isn't that going to an extreme?" But knowing David, he'd be the one to do just that; he didn't believe in doing things halfway.

"I'm done with women," he said, already world-weary at eighteen.

"I don't really like men, either," I said, opening my heart just a crack. David immediately turned his attention to me. "I mean, I've been hurt by my father in the past." I paused, emotional. As I unburdened my heart and began to share some of the unhappier memories of my childhood, David listened and didn't judge, which was odd, considering his personality at that time. I didn't cry or get emotional, but even so, I knew that whatever I said, David would be there for me.

"You know, I've got stories about my dad, too," he replied

when I had finished talking and began to tell me things he had told no one before. And while the swampy water swirled below us, we became more than just friends; we had become confidants.

2.6

So I made John's day by coming to the game, huh? Well, I'm glad I did. He asked me to be there, so I went, and I'm glad. I felt it was good for me to go. I'd have done it for anyone, though. I really didn't think it was that big of a deal.

You're not a guy, and you don't like him as much as he likes you, either.

What do you mean, guy? And what do mean, him liking me?

You are not a male (in gender), and you don't like him the way he likes you (a lot).

How does gender fit into this?

Don't ask. You're not a male.

I know that. But how does that. . . never mind. I won't ask what that has to do with anything. How are you? Happy, Happy, Joy, Joy.

Trudy, have you been watching Ren and Stimpy?

What does that have to do with anything?

Stimpy always says, "Happy, Happy, Joy, Joy."

I got the happy thing from my brother. I'm sorry for all my questions. I still don't get what all you were saying about gender stuff, but that's okay. Keep smiling!

I'll explain it. When a guy likes you a lot and asks you to do something, you can make his day by showing up.

I think I understand now. I didn't realize what my actions mean to him. We're not dating. Should I have not showed up? Am I leading him on?

No, he knows that it's over, but I think he still hopes.

AM I LEADING HIM ON?

I said no above. You can still be friends, but he will like you for a long time.

2.7

If I ever had a cross to bear, it was school. Unlike your father, who learned to read and write at the tender age of three, I took my time. Let's just say I took a very long time. I was so far delayed that I didn't start first grade until I was eight years old; even then I wasn't ready and struggled with reading, spelling, and math. Basically, you know, everything except recess. To top it off, the idea that a student could have learning disabilities was cutting-edge stuff in the school system when I was young, and resources were limited since I was going to a private, Seventh-day Adventist elementary school. But no matter how I tried, I couldn't make the marks on the page turn into words.

"Trudy, why can't you read?" my mother would chirp at me. "Your brother and sister both started reading younger than you and now you're in second grade. What's wrong with you!"

"I'm trying, Mom," I'd plead.

"You must need glasses," she decided. "I'm going to have to take you in to get examined."

But my eyes were, and still are, fine, but I still couldn't keep up with even the most basic aspects of school. Finally, realizing that something must be wrong, the administration brought in a special education teacher from a public school to assess me.

For three days, I sat alone in an empty classroom with the teacher as she asked me question after question. She dressed shabbily, and the smell of stale cigarette smoke on her clothes and breath nauseated me. She'd test me for hours until my brain ached, then give me far too short of a break so she could have a smoke before testing me again. Finally, after far too many questions, she came up with her diagnosis: I had a learning disability.

To this day, I can't tell you what my disability is. If the special ed teacher explained it to me, I can't remember what she said, and my family never talked about it, other than my mom's regular comments: "You'll never be able to get a college education with your learning disability," she'd decide for me. "And how could you be a nurse anyways? You'll make a mistake and kill someone. You know you will, Trudy. You're not safe."

After those assessments, nothing was done. I had no time with a special-ed teacher to learn how to learn, and my teachers, completely untrained, didn't provide any accommodations. However, one thing I do remember is that I needed to learn things three ways: I needed to hear it, read it, and write it down. That tip finally pushed me over the edge, and I slowly worked my way up from the bottom of my class. But I was on my own, and I had to work two or three times as hard to learn the same things as my classmates, while David could learn easily. To put it bluntly, school, the one thing everyone has to do, was hell for me.

And so it happened in November at Tacoma Baptist High School that I got my mid-term grades. I looked at the report card, saw that my hours and hours of hard work in Biology had earned me a D, and I lost it. The devastation was such a blow that as soon as class ended, I bolted to the girls' bathroom, locked myself in a stall, and sobbed, streaking my mascara until it ran into my blush. I had held it in for the class, but by now, I had moved into full freak-out mode. A few girls huddled around me with concern, asking me what was wrong, but soon the bell rang, and they apologetically rushed off to class. Only Jenny remained behind, halfway in and out the bathroom door, torn by her concern for me and being tardy for English.

At that moment, David walked down the hallway. It wasn't unusual for him to be wandering the hallways between classes. Every few weeks, he'd leave after a class and drive to Seattle for treatment for his rapidly worsening arthritis. He limped as he walked, leaning slightly on his cane. ("It's not a cane," he'd tell anyone who would listen. "It's a walking stick." And he'd promptly unscrew the cap, revealing a combination compass/sundial and a retractable flask filled with, oddly enough, lemon juice concentrate.)

Jenny, seeing David walking by, approached him with desperation in her eyes.

"Oh, David!" she said, already at the end of her rope. "I'm so glad it's you! Trudy is in the bathroom crying, and no one can make her stop. I'm already late for class and have to leave. But," she paused. "Maybe you can help her. She really needs someone."

"Okay," David said quickly. "You go to class, and I'll see what I can do."

As Jenny left, David took a half-second to consider his options, then knocked loudly on the bathroom door, catching me mid-wail.

"Hello?" he called. "Is there anyone other than Trudy in here?"

I tried to hold my breath and stay quiet. Only my loud sniffles gave me away. Another knock came.

"Trudy?" David's voice came through the cracked door.

"Go away!" I said in terror. "I don't want you to see me like this!" I curled further into the corner of the stall. Oh, the horror! David couldn't see me in this miserable and most vulnerable state. But where could I go? He was blocking the only exit. Fate was conspiring against me.

Slowly the door opened, revealing David, who immediately walked right into the stall, which, in my despair, I had neglected to lock. In my defense, I hadn't planned on a boy walking in on me.

"Trudy," David said gently. "What's going on?" He put his hand on my shoulder, our first touch other than that handshake over a year earlier.

"Don't talk to me," I blubbered. "I just want to die."

Then David, his hand still on my shoulder, turned my sobbing, hunched body towards him and held me closely.

"It's going to be okay," he told me. "Everything's going to be okay." I buried my head in his chest and cried myself dry, leaving his shirt damp and smeared with mascara.

Kids, you have to understand that in high school, everything is a big deal: like a Really Big Deal. You were spared the plight of every high school student I have met, if only because you were homeschooled. In high school, not homeschool, it's possible to live the very best and the worst day of your life within fifteen minutes. As David held me, all my worries left, and I slowly calmed down.

"How are you doing?" David said as my sobs eased to sniffles. He gently released me from his arms and looked me in the eyes.

I sniffed and looked in the mirror. "I can't go to class like this," I said as I wiped the mascara from my cheeks and started to break down again. "I can't do it, David." I began to sob. "I can't do this. It's too hard."

He wiped a tear from my cheek. "Come on." He took my hand. "School is almost over for the day, and then we can talk more."

Then he gently led me out of the bathroom and down the hallway until we stood in front of the door to English. "How are you doing?" he asked, checking with me again.

"I'm fine," I sniffled.

"You can do this, Trudy," he said. "I believe in you." Then he stepped back so no one in the classroom would see him when I entered. I turned, opened the door and walked in, my mind full of questions. *David didn't make fun of me,* I thought. *He believes in me. No one else has done that.* I sat down at my desk, trying to ignore all the girls' concerned looks. *He didn't think less of me. What on earth am I supposed to do with that?* At the moment, I felt peace, but later in the evening, panic set in. *David has seen me vulnerable! No one has seen me that vulnerable.* My mind reeled. Even though I didn't want to admit it, I needed help. No, I needed David. Yikes! I had never needed anyone like that before.

2.8

Dave,

I'm stuck! If John B. doesn't ask me to the Valentine's Banquet, John R. will! I don't know what to do. I don't want to hurt anyone. I could ask the dentist :) Hee, Hee, Hee!

Would you like to go with me? (No commitment, of course). You said that you wanted to have fun and I can do that. I hate to ask this early, but I'll do it to get you out of a jam. If you do say yes, I will have to say that I want it to be cheap. You game?

Of course, you could go with the dentist.

I don't want you to think that I was pressuring you to ask me because I wasn't. I was just talking about my predicament. But I would love to go with you to show everyone how to have fun! Please do keep it cheap. I only want to have fun. No pressures. Thanks, Dave! It'll be fun!

You didn't make me ask you. I needed a date anyways.

I still feel bad. I mean, I'm glad to get out of a tight spot, but still, I don't like to think I'm pressuring you. Strange, I know. But I think this is the first banquet that I'm just going to have fun. I don't have to worry about what he thinks of me, or what I think of him. You understand?

2.9

As we spent more and more time together, it became assumed that we were a couple. "But we're just friends," I protested to anyone who would listen. As we all knew, David was done with women, and I just assumed that I'd have to wait until college to find my soulmate.

But over time, despite our greatest efforts to keep it from happening, we began to fall in love.

2.10

Dear Dave,

I just finished my homework tonight and spent, oh, about ten minutes staring out my black window. Lots to see. I'm writing because you are on my mind a lot tonight. I don't know why, either. I think I'm trying to figure out the what you see is what you get Dave/David. All I know is that you are one of the most incredible people I have ever known. I have known a lot, more than you probably think, even. Yet you stand out of the crowd. You are a long way from understanding me, yet you are also closer than most.

You are like the first male that I've allowed myself to get close to. I think that it's because the pressure is off. We can have fun; we understand each other. Anyhow, I just have a lot of fun with you. I rely on you more than you'll ever know. You are my big brother, friend, listener/counselor, and emotional novio. I think you are really very special.

No wonder there are so many girls that like you. I know that there are much more than two, but they haven't verbally said so. Their eyes and hearts give many more away. I can't blame them;

you're a rare catch. Don't think that just because Susan spooked that they all do. You just had an unfortunate experience.

I love you, Dave. I truly do. I know that you are that person with a caring shoulder for me to literally cry on. The Lord placed you in my life during times I thought I couldn't go on. I'll never forget that knock on the girls' bathroom door, when you walked in to see me crying in a stall, all because I felt my whole life was over because of grades. I know that you had seen me in a very vulnerable state, and that scared me because people have hurt me in the past. But still, you have never let me down.

Thank you so much for your undying concern for my welfare. You mean the world to me. I pray that someday I will have the chance to repay you for the love you've shown me over the past few months. Through thick and thin you'll always be my friend, my brother, and my Dave.

2.11

Dear Trudy,

Today at work, I thought about love and what love was. I thought about the saying that love is an action, and I realized that I truly love you. Not the romantic, gushy kind of love, but the love of caring. Since I first had a chance to get to know you better at the beginning of October, you have become an integral part of my life. I have learned to rely on you, to lean on you when I can't stand. You have never failed me, and although I have really only known you for four months, I can say that I don't feel that you ever will. Yes, we make mistakes, but that isn't what I am talking about in the slightest. I am talking about the desire for another's best the entire time. You have exhibited that to me in the truest form. You have been a crutch in my life.

I cannot begin to tell you what you mean to me. I have been trying, but I am not sure how effective I have been. You have been there when I have questions, and you have been there to comfort me when I hurt. Yes, I have done whatever I can to help you, but that is because I want the best for you. I don't go to extremes to be of your service because I feel obligated to do so, but because I desire to do so. I have been able to open up to you in so many ways. You have taught me in ways that I have never seen before, and if I had seen them, only through you have they hit home.

I know that I have been quite diffuse, but I felt that I needed to tell you. Yes, I do love you, more than I can ever say. Thank you, Trudy. You have been a true blessing to me.

Happy Valentine's Day!

2.12

I had been David's friend, and things had worked out great, primarily because he wasn't interested in me. But when he professed his love for me in that Valentine's letter, I was stunned. I was full of barbs and stings for any guy who got too close, and easily could see through any of their advances. But David had done it all wrong. If he had tried to hit on me, I would have brushed him off. There was no way I would let any guy get away with those games. When I knew he wasn't into me, I relaxed and began to expose my vulnerable side to him. And now! Now love had snuck into it. It both blindsided and terrified me.

It was becoming more and more evident that we were clinging to the edge of an abyss, desperately trying to avoid disappearing in its depths. Each note we wrote only made it more obvious. We had to choose each word carefully. *How can I stay true to my heart and not lose a new best friend?* I spent hours pondering, trying to figure out a way to keep both. I had found a true friend in David; I even liked the way he always asked me what I was thinking every five seconds. He'd wrinkle his eyebrows in a question and then be actually interested in what I had to say. He seemed to truly value me: my thoughts, feelings, and our friendship. I'd never felt that way before; for most of my childhood, I had been dismissed and ignored.

I never got tired of seeing his face as he walked down the hallway, or catching the smell of his cologne by chance as we passed. And oh, there were his eyes: oversized, deep pools of dark-chocolate brown, they sleepily gazed into my soul. "Hey, Trudy?" he'd ask, his dark, limpid gaze looking my way, and I had to avoid eye contact because I'd lose my train of thought before I could answer. I could spend all day getting lost in them.

Was it possible he had any of these thoughts towards me? My mind twisted and turned, causing me to rapidly alternate between ecstasy and panic attacks. But I had to keep a poker face. I could not let him know how my heart skipped beats whenever I was near him. I had already told him too much, and opened my heart too much to him. *But if he loves me,* my mind kept reminding me. *If he really loves me...* Too mushy for you kids? Okay, Okay, I'll stop now. Here are some more notes proving how much we lied to ourselves to keep from being consumed by our love.

2.13

Dearest Trudy,

I just finished reading your letter again, and it meant much more to me the third time than the first. I just wanted to jot down some of my thoughts before they ran away.

I'm not sure if you feel this way, but it seems that we have grown incredibly close over the past few weeks. I don't know how to describe it, but I'll try. I am not romantically attracted to you at all (though you are very pretty), but the feelings that I feel towards you are almost like I am. Yet they are different. My heart is drawn very strongly to yours, and I literally feel with you. Not sympathy, but empathy. I have never met anyone quite like you. You are so special to me. We have such a unique friendship. You have such a heart for God. Did you know that your name means "Beloved of God"? Mine means the same thing. Maybe that is why we are so close. God has a plan for both of us. Keep that in mind.

Well, Trudy, it is dark now. I just felt I should write you.

2.14

Dearest Dave,

It still amazes me how much I have learned to trust in you. By now, you could truly hurt and destroy me, but I know you wouldn't. I trust in you like few others. Even when I was controlled by my state of pain and tears that freely flowed in the bathroom, and you showed up. I would not have planned for you to be there during that time. Yet God put you there, and there was nothing I could have done about it. During that time of vulnerability, I had peace with you there like no other. Mostly in the fact that you are male. There are things that I've not told you about me and men taking advantage of my vulnerable heart. I'm sorry, Dave, I don't feel too good right now, and I am crying. But I don't think I'll scribble out what I wrote about men.

Oh boy, I need to talk to you in person about this one. I don't trust paper any more. It will be hard for me, though. No, I don't trust men; I used to hate them even. Now I just hurt. I'm reliving old hidden emotions stored up from long ago.

I'm sorry, Dave, I'll have to go further in private. I think that through you, God is healing me from many things in my past. Thank you for your strength and encouragement.

2.15

Trudy,

Hello! You know I have a locker next to you, and I write you notes almost every day in Bible, but it seems like I never talk to you. Is it me, or am I loopy?

I know! I think that I am feeling feelings of mad, passionate, unbridled friendship towards you. That's it!

You are too loopy for me, Dave. But it is true that it seems like we never do talk. Thanks for putting a smile on my face. You keep me going. My imagination has really taken off since I've known you. Thanks for teaching me how to be me!

On another note, why don't we get married, so we can see each other more often? You know, it could be a friendship type of marriage.

Yeah, Dave, whatever, okay, Dave. Let's get married. It would be a unique marriage. I've never heard of a friendship type of marriage. It would be different. But what should I do about the dentist? Maybe I could marry him, too! You know, the other marriage :)

Ah, but Trudy, that would be adultery! I can't believe that you would be unfaithful to me! Where is your heart, you puppet of Satan?

But I thought it was a friendship marriage.

Sorry, I didn't know that visiting the dentist brought up such strong feelings in you. Do you have sensitive teeth?

No, Dave, my teeth are not sensitive. But John doesn't know about the dentist. I'd just rather not have him know, especially when it's not really even serious. It's more of a joke. Don't worry about it, though.

I'd be worried if I had my teeth worked on by a good-looking, affable dentist that was hitting on me. Are you going to ask him?

No, I most likely won't see him anyway. I'm just getting them cleaned. If I do see him, I still will not talk to him because it's probably all in my head.

Can we still get married? (As friends, that is)

2.16

It felt like fate's ever-present pull kept tugging at us, inexorably moving us closer together. But we lied to ourselves out of the best intentions. We were just friends who happened to also love each other–you know, the friendship kind of love. The illusion really only worked for us. David and I had become inseparable, and everyone thought of us as a couple. Teachers mid-semester suddenly changed the seating arrangements, separating David and me to the far corners of our classrooms in a vain and fruitless attempt to keep us from passing notes.

"You were looking at David with googly eyes all day in class," a friend told me as we packed up our books from Miss Teague's English.

"What!" I half-yelled. "I was *not!*"

"Yeah, whatever, Googly Eyes," she teased.

Over and over, I swore that we were just friends until I actually believed it.

That is, until an unusually warm April day in the Spring of 1994. The scene looked like this: The sun slowly faded into the mist of the Olympic Mountains, the afternoon slowly turning toward twilight. A picnic blanket stretched out on the edge of a cliff that dropped a hundred feet down toward the saltwater of Puget Sound. Off in the distance, a container ship threaded its way through the Narrows of Puget Sound, leaving a frothy white wake that shone for a moment before disappearing into the whitecaps. David sat to my right, a couple of feet away, his legs dangling over the cliff.

"You know, Trudy." His smooth chocolatey voice broke the silence of the stillness. He brushed his hands over the small, new grass poking out of the ground beside him. "You know I have feelings for you. You know I love you."

The silence returned again. I knew what he was going to say, and I desperately craved it with all of my being. But I was scared, scared of what his words would mean to me, to us. Scared of getting hurt and hurting him. Scared of falling in love with my best friend. I held my hands tight in my lap, desperately wanting him to finish his thought.

"What if we take all that, we have now, you know, the friendship, the fun times, and all that. What if we keep all that and just admit that we are falling in love? But we take it slow, like real slow."

He said it! He finally said what I felt and had been trying to deny for months. Instead of anxiety, I felt joy, like part of me had come alive. I took a deep breath; the cool, damp air filled my lungs and dissolved my fears.

"You mean we don't have to lose our friendship? We can just admit to being what everyone says we are, a couple?" I said, relieved. The container ship had pulled out of the Narrows by now and was working its way north towards Tacoma and Seattle, leaving its speckled wake behind.

"Yes. But we need to take it slow. I don't trust myself and the feelings I have for you." He paused. "I mean that we have for each other."

There was no denying it; in the past months, our love had already grown far more than I had imagined or dreamed possible. I was feeling things I had never felt before. Slowly, David was becoming my obsession, not by choice but because he consumed every fiber of my consciousness. Even in my dreams, he was near. He had given me his childhood teddy bear and sprayed it with his cologne. It slept with me at night, and I held it tight, thinking of David and how he cared for me. I gave him my teddy bear to care for in exchange. There was no doubt that love had enslaved us to its torment and delight. We were helplessly intoxicated to it, its will, and its power.

"Yes, I think that would be okay," is all I could say. How could I say more for fear of losing my composure? Nothing would change; it was still us, our friendship, and just a little bit more. But despite my barking fears, I felt a peace I had never known. *This has to be right*, I thought, *because nothing has ever felt more right than this moment, than us.*

"Trudy," David once again interrupted my straying thoughts, "May I put my arm around you, then?" We had never touched other than that hug when he pulled me out of the girls' bathroom. So kids, Tacoma Baptist High School had a strict policy of absolutely no physical contact with the opposite sex. But we'll talk more about sex, the other kind of sex, later.

"Yes," I responded before I had a chance to mull it over and listen to my fears. "I think that would be alright." Gently, he took his left arm, reached around my back, and pulled me close. As he squeezed me near, I leaned into him, resting my head on his shoulder. An undeniable warmth and peace filled me; my fears and anxiety lifted and blew away, carried across the water and into the deepening sunset. We didn't say much as time ticked by, his arm around me. What felt like holy silence enveloped us in a moment that will forever remain timeless.

But even timeless moments end. The sun had long sunk behind the mountains, and dusk had rapidly turned to nighttime. Reluctantly, we folded up David's picnic blanket, walked away from the cliff, and down the trail. But as we walked back to the cars, his hand gently reached for mine. As my fingers wrapped around his, I saw in a flash our lives together. I saw a home, a baby in a crib, a life, and a family. I knew this was only the beginning of a lifelong romance filled with adventure.

A few moments later, we were standing in the parking lot. David had parked next to my car, delaying our inevitable separation. The parking lot lights overhead gave off a warm glow, framing us in a circle of light amidst the deepening night. David put his hand on my cheek and stared at me.

"You're so beautiful, Trudy Ann Lanette Pflugrad," he said in delight, as if seeing me for the first time. Perhaps he was seeing me for the first time. I was all new inside, knowing I had found what I had been looking for my whole life: the rest of me, the other half of my soul. I had embraced it with my whole being the moment he reached for me. I could accept him and all of his love for me wholeheartedly, without fear.

His eyes filled with tears, but he couldn't look away. He trembled ever so slightly as he gently caressed my hair, my neck, my jawline. Then he placed his hand on my cheek once again and pulled me towards him, looking into my eyes. "You're so beautiful," he repeated, "like a goddess."

And just like that, things forever changed between us. For better or worse, it was the beginning of us as a couple.

CHAPTER III

IN WHICH
Your Mother and Father Discover the Hard Way to Kill a Cat

3.1

Dearest Trudy,

I thank you again for the wonderful evening on Saturday. I can't even begin to express what it meant to me. When you told me you love me, it hurt, but it was a wonderful hurt. You mean an awful lot to me.

I accept you for who you are, Trudy. I accept your weaknesses, your faults, your imperfections. They make you who you are, the wonderful you.

3.2

Dearest Dave,

All I know is that my feelings are very much undefined. I know that I truly did love you even before Saturday night. I just don't exactly know what I feel right now. I kinda want to cry. I hate seeing you at school now because I don't know how to look at you. I want to talk to you in person, Dave. I want to settle all this stuff.

I'm treating you like nothing has changed. I'm all out of whack. I am so unsure and afraid of my feelings right now. In all honesty, I'm scared to death. I don't know what's going on. I think I'm seeing you like I saw you Saturday night, but at school, you're the same person.

I do need to tell you that although I am very scared also, I would never hurt you. David, I want to be the one that heals, loves, and helps you to grow. How can I help you? How can I take away your fear, pain and sorrow?

I never in my wildest dreams would have seen the two of us like this. . . together. It simply amazes me, you. You, of all people! I never would have thought you could see me as you do. You see and understand me in a way that really no other one person ever could.

I think that God is showing me how to have and express these emotions of loving and caring for someone, especially a male. I do not trust males at all. I don't know why, except for the two stories that I told you. Having these feelings towards you that go beyond a friendship is very much intimidating to me. But God has literally thrust you into my life at the most vulnerable times. Do you know what that means to me? A great deal, that's what. I think you are going to heal my scars and take away my fears.

3.3

Being a couple only changed the way David and I saw each other. No one else knew anything was different. They already assumed we were dating; it just took us a while to realize that we actually were. And once we did, it was a relief to be able to say what we felt and to share our hopes, dreams, and the possibility of a life lived together. We became inseparable both at school and off campus. Every free afternoon or weekend, we were together. And when we weren't together, we monopolized our home phones to the point of both sets of parents itemizing our minutes and charging us monthly. Because we lived in different area codes, we had to pay for long-distance, which quickly added up. So, we wrote more letters; we've got hundreds of pages of notes from our years of high school.

David soon learned that if he helped me study for tests and we did homework together, I got it done so much faster and we could have even more time with each other. I was grateful because no matter how hard I tried, school was a torment in my life, and David knew exactly how to explain things to me in a way I could actually learn and remember. It helped that we had many classes together. I was in love with him teaching me, his furrowed eyebrows earnestly checking to see if I was understanding what he was saying before quizzing me. I loved the shape of his hands, calloused enough to know hard work but so soft when he handled textbook pages, and gentle when he touched my arm when exchanging a book. I loved watching him while I learned, and my grades improved.

Nothing could be more perfect. We were meant for each other. Oh, but there was one thing: Religion. Yup, kids, God was the decisive difference between us. I was Seventh-day Adventist, remember, so it was unimaginable that I would *ever* go to church on Sunday, no matter how much I loved David.

David, on the other hand, couldn't figure out some of the more esoteric Adventist doctrines, particularly Ellen G. White, the one and only prophet of the Seventh-day Adventist church. She had visions and prophecies about everything from heaven (good) to caffeine (bad) to masturbation (really bad). But it didn't matter what stories I had heard about the "Pen of Inspiration," as my pastor called her. David was brutal and inflexible when it came to what he considered "issues of truth." While I could talk about the philosophy of the process, David chose to "discuss" issues on his terms, using Greek and Hebrew references, thirty different books, and details, details, details. He would have considered anything less than this vigorous attack a compromise of his faith.

"So, she was a prophet," he re-opened a conversation with me one day after school. We had been hashing out this topic every time we were alone, along with other "key doctrinal issues."

"Yes," I replied, "I believe that she was." David had taken to giving me book after book exposing the false doctrines of Seventh-day Adventism, so I had given him a copy of Ellen White's *The Great Controversy*. Not that I had ever read it, but I figured if anyone could figure it out, David could.

"If she was a prophet, then her prophecies would have come true, right?" he posited, leading me in his argument.

"Well, yes, I believe that they were."

"But what about this one?" he probed. "Look." He pulled out a thick book filled with small print. "She said that an angel told her that some people in 1856 would live to see Jesus' return. Listen to this: 'Some food for worms, some subjects of the seven last plagues, some will be alive and remain upon the earth to be translated at the coming of Jesus.' He looked up smugly, certain his argument was airtight. "I know they're all dead now."

"Well," I gave an inch. "Just because one of her prophecies didn't come true doesn't mean she wasn't a prophet."

"What about this?" David flipped a few more pages. "She says wigs cause insanity. Here it is: 'Covering the base of the brain, [wigs] heat and excite the spinal nerves centering in the brain. . . many have lost their reason and become hopelessly insane.' That's just not true."

"But some of her prophecies came true," I said. "She was a prophet."

"Okay," David went along with me, playing Devil's Advocate. "Let's say she was a prophet. There are lots of prophets in the Bible. So, if she was a prophet, why aren't there any more in the Adventist Church? Is she the only one?"

And on and on and on it went. It was a big deal to us because we were grappling with issues that, in our mind, were of eternal importance. Was it worth it to go to hell for love? Not for David or me. In fact, religion caused the first of our many breakups. But don't worry. We never could break up for long before we ran back into each other's arms.

3.4

Trudy,

What if some of my questions can't be answered?

Does any church have all the truth? Can you accept it if your questions aren't answered? This is a mental workout which I am not going to stop until it is over.

There is no church that has all the right answers. You will have to prove the doctrines wrong for me to change. No, I don't think that our church or any church has the right answers. Only time will be the judge. I put God first. I have to.

3.5

My Beloved,

Is our relationship on hold still, or is "our" decision just not finalized?

As far as I'm concerned, we're not on hold. I also am trying to remain open. I'll listen to anything you have to say.

Can you hear me if I say, "I love you"?

Yep

3.6

Of course, love won out, and our doctrinal differences didn't tear us apart. David compromised on some things, and I compromised on others, sometimes with disconcerting results.

It was Christmas, and I couldn't imagine a happier holiday season. What could possibly make Christmas merrier? Being in love, of course. It was lunchtime at school, and this being our senior year, we had the privilege of going off campus for the lunch break. For couples, this was code for leaving campus to break the "no touching the opposite sex" rule, and David and I took full advantage of that privilege. We learned that we could drive off campus, park half a block away in an alley, and have all the privacy we needed to make out passionately before returning to school, David wearing half my makeup. Sometimes we also ate lunch.

"So, Trudy," began David between bites of his ham sandwich. "Do you believe eating unclean meat is truly a sin?"

"I believe there is clean and unclean meat, just like the Bible says," came my curious response. As a lifelong Adventist, I avoided all meat, not just pork and shellfish.

"But it's not like a salvation kind of sin, is it?" he continued.

I had to think about that for a moment. "Why eat something that you already know is bad for your body?" I said, inwardly revolted at the look, smell, and very idea of pork or shellfish.

"Yeah, but you won't go to hell for it, though." I couldn't argue that point. Even I had to admit it was a dietary preference. I took a bite of my apple in curiosity, knowing David was up to something, that he was going to compromise me in some way.

"Well, I want to take you out to Red Lobster so you can eat seafood just once in your life." He didn't even pause for my panic attack. "You won't die; I promise," he said as he leaned towards me with his mischievous and equally stubborn smile.

"But what about food poisoning! Did you know shellfish is one of the greatest causes of foodborne illnesses?" I exclaimed in horror and disgust, repeating words drilled into my head from childhood.

David belly laughed so hard I thought I had missed something. *It can't be what I said,* I thought and turned my head to see what was happening outside that was so funny. He continued to guffaw until I realized: *He is laughing at me.* I turned pale, and butterflies filled my stomach.

"Trudy," David said, leaning into me once he finally stopped giggling. "Thousands of people eat at Red Lobster every day. They know how to cook food properly; it's their job."

I looked down, not willing to concede my point just yet. I mean, there had to be some way out of this dilemma.

"I've eaten there numerous times and never once got sick, and I don't know anyone who has gotten sick. I promise you it will be okay." His gentle voice tried to soothe my stress, and he took my hand in his, reassuring me. David wasn't making fun of me at all. He simply wanted me to trust him with one more of life's many adventures. But hey, I finally was going to get a meal out of him! In the end, I reluctantly accepted his offer.

So, it happened one Saturday evening in mid-December that I found myself looking at a fish tank full of lobsters in the lobby of Red Lobster while holiday music played in the background. Merry people chattered amongst themselves, undoubtedly hungry and eager for their, *ugh*, seafood meal.

"Why do they have rubber bands around their claws?" I whispered to David, fixated in a trance of disgust on the lobster tank. My stomach, although quite empty and hungry, turned sour.

The door opened, and I swung around quickly, frantically checking to see if it was someone I knew. No one, absolutely no one, at home, knew what I was doing–my great compromise and sin. I just knew I would be found out and forever shamed. Interestingly, the thought never occurred to me that if I had seen someone from church, we would both be caught in this great evil. Nope, I was more concerned about my sin and knew I couldn't hide from God. The happy, rosy-cheeked faces stepped out of the rain and found the other half of their dinner party near the fake Christmas tree. I sighed in relief. I didn't recognize any of them, and most importantly, no one seemed to recognize me. I was safe and resumed my previous stare at the tank, full of what perhaps would be my future meal. Oh, the thought! I shuddered.

"What are you talking about?" David looked around the room in bewilderment. My finger lifted toward the tank and poked at the glass. He followed my gaze, then realized I had never seen such a sight. "Oh, they put rubber bands around their claws so they don't pinch anyone's fingers before they're cooked," he said like it was no big deal.

I breathed in the salty, steamy air of the restaurant, and my stomach turned again. Diners everywhere were cracking shells and throwing them on their tables, digging into the body cavities of these helpless creatures, eviscerating them, and then *eating their flesh.* I had a hard time breathing. My eyes looked longingly towards the restaurant's door; there lay my salvation and fresh, cool, clean air. *Perhaps I can convince him to leave,* I thought, just a second too late.

"David, party of two? Your table is ready!" came a happy voice from the opposite direction of the door. Instinctively and against my better judgment, I followed the smiling face to a table.

"Here's your menu. Your server will be with you shortly," she said in a saccharin voice. I smiled out of politeness, my stomach churning inside. David, being the romantic, had thought of everything. Within moments a chilled bottle of sparkling apple cider was brought to the table. David and his huge cow eyes looked into mine reassuringly. The gesture was sweet and thoughtful; for half a moment, I forgot I was in seafood hell.

I opened the menu, and everything looked disgusting. "So, do you want shrimp?" he asked. "Lots of people like shrimp."

I shrugged.

"Crab? Lobster? Oysters?"

I wasn't listening. I was too busy scanning the tables around me to see if I saw someone from church.

"You know what?" he said. "How about we get the sampler platter? Then we'll get a bit of everything."

Gratefully I set down the menu. As David placed the order, I did one more scan of the restaurant, double-checking to make sure I didn't know anyone. I settled down a bit more. Until tables changed their patrons, I was safe. *It's odd*, I thought, *that all the people around me are eating this food and thinking nothing of it, like they are the normal ones and I'm the looney in the room.*

All too soon, the massive platter showed up, filled with crab, lobster (oh, how I hoped it wasn't one of the ones I had seen earlier), shrimp, clams, scallops, oysters, and wonderfully, bread! I eagerly reached for a roll, hoping to soothe my sour stomach before I prepared it for something so much worse. David unfolded an oversized napkin and put it in his lap, and then, weirdly, he began to unfold an oversized plastic bib!

"What on earth is this for? I thought. *What, do they think I'm two again?* I looked around the room and saw many other patrons proudly wearing bibs as if being a toddler is the norm for seafood, so I dutifully followed suit. *At least it puts off the inevitable a little longer.* Then David, eager to begin, grabbed a hammer and began beating on a huge crab leg, making it look as natural as cracking a walnut shell. My eyes widened, but he was just getting going. Then he took a long, narrow fork and began pulling out the strange, pale, smelly flesh inside. My stomach had gone into revolt, but I couldn't put off eating much longer without making a scene.

"It's alright," David said, taking a bite and handing me my own crab leg to pulverize and consume. No matter how I tried, I couldn't figure out how to properly crack the crab legs. *It's their last revenge,* I thought, *making you have to work to get to their flesh.* I poked, pried, and pulled, and soon the deed was done. I held the wobbly, stringy meat on my fork and looked at it.

"Dip it in the butter," David said. "It's better that way." He motioned to the small silver dish sitting on the side of the oversized platter of Satan's food. I dipped, took a bite, and chewed. I had never eaten anything vaguely like it. It tasted nothing like Skallops or Tuno, the soy alternatives for seafood I had grown up with. I chewed three, four, five times and swallowed.

"See," David smiled. "It's not so bad."

And just then, I kid you not, there was an earthquake. The noise in the restaurant had quieted the boom that is often heard before the shake, making the shake that much more shocking. The windows chattered, distorting the wet, western Washington blackness just outside. People looked around the room. "Is that an earthquake?" a woman asked nearby, and a few people pushed back chairs and began to crawl under their tables. Just as I was ready to duck and cover, the shaking stopped, causing no damage other than a few toppled crab legs.

I knew God had found me out.

"David." My eyes widened. "I shouldn't be here."

David laughed, trying to gloss over God's judgment. "It's nothing," he said. "I'm sure it's no big deal." He ate a few more scallops, and I poked at some shrimp and tried the clams. *At least*, I thought, *the evening was not an utter failure. I had an adventure*, I reassured myself. *And I will never have to sin again.* I proved I could eat unclean meat.

But the evening wasn't over yet.

3.7

Soon we were in the relative shelter of David's Hot Wheels-sized Samurai.

"I thought we'd look at Christmas lights," he announced, putting in a CD. With dinner now safely behind me, his company filled me with delight.

"Of course," I replied. "That sounds like fun."

Moments later, and about twenty decibels too loud, the Christmas music started. It wasn't Nat King Cole singing *The Christmas Song*, Bing Crosby crooning *White Christmas*, or anything I would associate with the holidays. Nope. He had picked Gregorian Christmas chants. While the tiny little car bumped down the freeway, the voice chanted in high, nasal, and extremely loud Latin. The music took me by surprise but strangely agreed with the thing that David had going. I settled into the slightly odd holiday cheer as we made our way down the hills of Tacoma toward the twinkling lights surrounding Puget Sound. As we drove by the warmly lit homes, I imagined family and friends gathering together, making happy holiday memories.

"I know of a few places that should be pretty," David said as he turned down a street. "My grandparents live not too far from here." He slowed the car so we could take in the glittering lights. The never-ending, damp, Western Washington drizzle, combined with our rain-dampened clothes, fogged up the windows to his less-than-airtight vehicle. A snowman waved silently at us as we drove past. David took my hand out of his and reached to turn on the defrost. Suddenly we felt a hard bump under the tires. We had hit something.

David looked into the rearview mirror as he pulled the car to the curb and parked. "I have to see what I ran over," he said as he opened the door and got out. I sat calmly, wondering what indeed he had hit. We hadn't seen anything obvious. A few seconds later, he came back and sat in the driver's seat, raindrops covering his hair and jacket.

"It's a cat, Trudy. I ran over a cat." David jerked his jeep into reverse, turning it around. "It's still alive. I just broke its back." He lined up the Samurai and aimed. "I'm so sorry," he apologized in advance. "I have to kill it. I can't let it suffer." He stepped on the gas, and the same *bump bump* under the tires happened again.

"It's still not dead!" David exclaimed in horror as he watched the cat flop on the roadway behind us. He swung the Samurai around and had another go.

Bump bump, went the tires a third time, then a fourth. By now, David had realized the truth. His lighter-than-air Suzuki Samurai couldn't get the job done. He popped out and looked at the now disfigured cat.

"I'm so sorry, Trudy," David repeated as he dug around in the back for a tire iron. "Its back is severely broken, and I can't kill it any other way," his voice said a little shakily. He took the tire iron in hand, walked over to the half-crushed feline, and bashed its head in, finally finishing what the Samurai couldn't. He pushed the cat's body to the curb, walked through the drizzle to the nearest house, and knocked on the door. A few minutes later, he came back.

"They don't know whose cat it is," he said, disheartened, as he put the bloody tire iron away. "And there's no collar, so I can't call the owners. What else can we do?" He gloomily climbed back in and sat for a while before driving off. But we didn't get too far; all the cat-mauling had given him a flat tire.

David sighed as he pulled off of the highway, parked, and pulled out the blood-stained tire iron. Once again, I sat in the car as he got progressively damper, changing the flat on the side of Highway 16. After a half-hour he climbed in, completely wet and disheartened.

"Not the best date, huh," he said, putting it in first and pulling back into traffic.

It would take years for me to eat shellfish again.

Trudy Wakefield

3.8

Even though David and I had worked things out, our families had their own ideas of our futures; neither saw converting to another denomination as an option. My father, in particular, refused to acknowledge my relationship with a Baptist boy.

"You know how hard it is for me to apologize," he told me as we waited in the car for my mom to finish her shift at the nursing home.

I didn't acknowledge his statement, but I kept listening, fixing my eyes hard on the trees in front of our parked car. The damp air lofted through the open windows, bringing a hint of saltwater to fill the car along with my silence. His tense, shaky voice continued, reading my non-verbals.

"Your mom said if I didn't apologize, you'd run away with David, and we'd never see you again."

My continued silence confirmed both my mom's worst fears and my father's suspicions. But was this actually my dad trying to apologize? It felt more like him trying to see how much he could get away with. Only a day ago, he had yelled me down, demanding that I break up with David. You see, David was no closer to converting to Adventism than I was to becoming a Baptist, and this worried my father. His daughter leaving the church for love simply was not an option, and he did what he always had done in the past to enforce his rule of law in our home: he ranted, raved, and threatened.

Flashes of his angry, unfair words about David flew through my mind. His hovering, hollering rage still rang in my ears. My sister tried to sink into the living room couch. Realizing that wouldn't work, she disappeared upstairs. My mom watched him yell, occasionally interjecting a "Lester" now and again, trying to break his barrage of words that pierced like bullets. I took all of it because I had to then. I had nowhere else to live. But no, I could not, and would not, forget. He was in the wrong, and my mind was made up.

I sat in silence. My eyes told him everything he needed to know: I was still angry, and he hadn't fixed anything yet. He would have to do a better job. Worry softened his clenched fists as he saw for the first time that I was not afraid of him. I sighed loudly and jerked the car door open.

"I'm done," I proclaimed as I rose out of the car and began walking toward the nursing home door. He quickly followed me.

"You know how hard it is for me to apologize," he repeated as he intercepted my steps.

I paused, looking at him. "Yes," I said, waiting for him to actually apologize.

"Well, I'm sorry," he huffed, "And I don't think I've ever apologized to anyone before, not even your mother." There, he said it. Whether it was out of desperation, fear, or just trying to avoid the consequences of his rage, he said it. That was supposed to be a big deal, the greatest sacrifice of his adult life.

I had no words. Was I supposed to feel resolved or grateful for his supposed self-sacrifice? I felt confused. Was I heard? Did he understand how much he had hurt me? It was obvious he had nothing more to give me or to say. But the apology made nothing right. I knew he had not changed, that he still thought the same way about us. He was just apologizing because he got caught. *This is as good as he's going to get.* The thought rolled across my mind. I paused again, knowing I was already the more mature adult in this conversation.

"Thank you," I stated flatly, more to get him to stop bothering me than anything else.

Light filled his lusty eyes, and a gleeful smile crossed his face, the same look that he always had when he got what he wanted.

I turned away from him and walked into the nursing home. He followed behind. My face looked down the long hallway toward my resolve. *How soon can I get out of this home?* I asked myself. I did not let his steps catch up to mine.

Your mom approves.

But that's different!

You said that it was okay just a second ago, so let's do it. I won't tell.

3.11

My Own Beloved,

I guess I should be still studying, but it's after 9 pm and my brain and eyes are strained. The battle was fierce today. I know it's to be expected, though. I was having too many good days for it to last forever.

I think this whole thing started with #1, exhaustion, and #2, second period. It hit me how hard I'm going to have to study for this Mythology test. Even though I know that I will study for all I'm worth, I still know the outcome. So why even try? If I'm going to flunk, why waste my time studying?

It's true. I am stupid and ignorant. Most teachers think of me as a slacker. I'm too proud to make excuses and tell them about my "learning disabilities." What a JOKE! I may be learning disabled, but I do have pride. Is that wrong? What makes me less of a person than someone else? Mental problems are always looked down on. Now I'm crying. I'm sorry. I hate to drag you through this. But I promised.

And then you call me wonderful. How can you? It's almost an insult to me. How can you say that when I listed all those things about myself? I'm so confused. If God made me this way, then why can't the world accept me? Why can't I be me? I cannot, cannot conform to the world's standards. I try, oh how I try, but I remain the fool.

It hurts so bad. I long so much to be near you. I can almost feel you holding me close. I need you, David. I'm tired of being alone. But I can't allow you to be caught in the Trudy trap. You can't put up with me. Yet the harder I fight you, the more I fall in love with you.

I'm so sorry, David. I'd understand if you left me. In fact, I'd feel better if you did. I'm weighing you down and I am oh so sorry. Yet why do I love you so much? I'd give anything to be with you. My, I sure do go from one extreme to the other. Leave me, stay with me. I'm truly messed up. If you can figure out this mess, what my feelings are, then you truly are a remarkable person. Then again, you are anyway. Thanks for your patience.

Your fellow warrior,

Trudy

3.12

Dearest,

I wanted to thank you for your letter. I am not going to condemn you or leave you simply because I can't. You mean too much to me. I respect you for being open to sharing your feelings with me. I want to encourage you as much as I can. I won't let you give up. I have seen your heart, and I cannot help but be amazed, Trudy.

I have been daydreaming a lot about our castle in the sky. I would love to fall asleep in your arms. You have such wonderful arms. I could write an epic poem about your hands. There is nothing like your touch. You speak a thousand words without saying a thing.

You are so much a part of my life. It is almost as if I am you. I feel your pain, I hurt with you. I am yours. Please let me take care of you. I have to. I love you. I don't have a choice. If I did have one, I would do everything the same. I am too attached to you, like a barnacle on a rock. You are so amazing. I respect you a lot, my beloved.

Trudy Wakefield

3.13

Dearest Beloved,

Just a quick note to say thank you for helping me. 96%! I can hardly believe I did that! Wow! :) Thank you. I give you the credit.

It's just that I'm too proud to admit needing your help. You know my needs far too well for me to argue with you. There lies my problem. I think I've fallen in love and I don't know what to do. Where would I be without you? I don't even want to think of that.

Why can't I get rid of this feeling that I can't be happy? That I'm not meant to be happy? I've never truly been happy before. Why now? Something bad will happen to take it away from me. I don't deserve it. It almost scares me and keeps me from wanting to be happy at all. I'm all messed up.

There's no one else quite like you. Your love means the world to me. You have all the love I can give. Oh, I'm also very glad that you don't call me "Babe." It was the nickname John gave me. I HATED IT! You are just too wonderful, too perfect for me. You could call it a match made in heaven. I like that idea.

Caring for you,
Trudy

3.14

Trudy,

You are so wonderful. I love you dearly.

Were you able to write my mom? I am sure that she would like a visit from you. You could visit her some day after school. It's just an idea, not a plan.

3.15

"Would you like a glass of water, Trudy?" asked my future mother-in-law.

"Sure. That sounds nice," I replied, smiling.

David had been sent downstairs a few minutes before so that Lilith and I could have "a little heart-to-heart." I sat in an overstuffed chair in his family's expansive living room. Sun glinted off the lake and through the wall of windows that covered the front of the house. While she puttered in the kitchen, I looked at the large brick fireplace, above which hung pictures of David and his family. She returned, carrying a glass cup filled with water, looking at me down her beaked nose. We exchanged pleasantries and talked about my date with David when the mood of the room suddenly changed.

"Well, Trudy," she began, suddenly taking the conversation in a completely different direction, "Now that your relationship is getting more serious with my son, I thought we should have a little heart-to-heart and get to know each other better." She smiled, but her eyes didn't seem happy. My heart began to pound in my chest as a sense of uneasiness came over me. I couldn't understand what it was that was making me feel so uncomfortable and nervous.

"Okay," I said cautiously, but not giving myself away. I uncrossed my legs and took a slow, deliberate sip of water as she continued.

"I think you are good for David, much better than Susan was. She just never was very deep, and I couldn't really connect or talk with her like I can you." Her eyes narrowed, and she offered me another consolatory smile. I simply smiled back, choosing to appear shy and timid instead of responding to her. This seemed to work as her eyes relaxed more, and she leaned back, her short stature dwarfed by her oversize chair.

"Well," she went on, choosing not to wait for my response to her over-obvious compliment to me and insult to my still-best friend. "You know David has a special calling and purpose in his life, don't you, Trudy?"

"Yes, I know. He has talked to me about it before." I replied, trying to hide my nervousness and shaky voice. I had no idea where this was going, and I felt very afraid. But I still couldn't understand why.

"Yes," she replied. "Well, he was prophesied over while he was still in my womb. I was told I was carrying a son and to name him David." She paused. "He has a high destiny and has been called to be a great leader." There was a fondness in her voice as though she were reliving the beauty of that moment.

"Yes, he told me that, too." I said simply, smiling encouragingly. What David thought about these "prophecies" didn't matter. Perhaps I didn't fully understand the importance of these facts or how much of a bearing they would have on my life because she leaned toward me, her eyes narrowing as she scrutinized every part of my being, searching me to see if I was suitable enough material for her son. All the smiles and pleasantries were gone. As she assessed me, I saw an orange-red light begin to glow from behind her, as if she were surrounded by fire. It terrified me. Then she spoke.

"Well," she paused, clicking her tongue. "I know that you have dreams and plans for your future." For a brief moment, I actually thought she was talking about me and my aspirations. "But understand that these plans can never get in the way of David's purpose for his life. You are to come alongside him and be a helpmate to him so that he may achieve his destiny. Do you understand this?"

Ahh, this wasn't about me in the least. In fact, it seemed that I wasn't even a person to her. I nodded, shocked by her sudden candidness. She had stunned me into almost dropping my guard, but I held onto my glass of water, looking at the refracted living room in its light.

Lilith's eyes burrowed into me like a searchlight. "If you ever get in the way of his calling." Here she paused, making sure that what she said sunk in. Then she spoke slowly and

3.9

You are my Psyche.

How was your morning? I was telling my mom about going with you on the trip. She said that I should go. I just thought you'd like to know that. :)

In Bible you need to write a one-page paper on a day of Paul's life growing up. Due Monday. It's good to see you.

So, your mom approves of us running away together? Thanks for the assignment.

Sounds like it :)

Are you busy after school?

My mom is picking me up.

We could leave a ransom note.

I don't know how that would go over.

clearly. "I will make your life a living hell." She leaned back in her chair, full of intensity. She had said her peace. It felt like one of those scenes from a mobster movie. You know, the ones where the newcomer sits down and gets to know "the family." The real purpose of this heart-to-heart finally became clear. That was the cause of my anxiety and heart pounding. My mind narrowed to a pinpoint of focus. I had to get out of here in one piece. *But how?* I thought to myself. In a moment, I knew who she really was and that I could have nothing to do with her in my life. I cared for David. I loved him. But I wanted nothing to do with this kind of crazy. In my mind, it was over. I managed to grow a smile on my face as I replied.

"I would never try to get in the way of his calling," I said sweetly. Relief washed over her face, and the red glow dispersed around her as her body once again relaxed.

"That's good. Now, why don't you go downstairs and find David? I'm sure he's been wondering about you and our little chat," she said happily as she sprang up from her chair. It was over, and I had survived.

I walked down the stairs and turned into the family room, where I saw David sitting on the couch, reading a book.

"Well, how was your time?" he asked brightly, then seeing my face shifted to concern. "Are you okay?"

"Yeah. But I need to go right now," I said.

Not at all convinced, he studied my face. "Let's go get some yogurt downtown before you head home," he offered.

"Okay," I simply replied, relieved to go absolutely anywhere to tell him what I had to say and end it all. I collected my things and walked up the stairs to the entry as David told his mom he'd be back later.

"Have fun, you two!" she said happily, heading back into the kitchen.

3.16

The bright yellow paint couldn't warm the inside of the oversized building that housed the yogurt shop. Perhaps once it had been nice, but now it looked worn and beaten and felt more like an industrial space than a sweet shop. The place was frigid; maybe they didn't want any lingering customers or were trying to save money on refrigeration. My fingers turned red as we got our yogurt. Maybe a frozen treat on a chilly day wasn't the best idea.

Our chairs squeaked as they scraped on the hard tile floor, echoing in the cold space. I spoke quietly as if I was afraid someone might be listening, even though the shop was dead empty.

"I don't think things are going to work out for us," I said while David took his first bite. He looked up at me. "I mean, I don't think I can continue to date you," I said, completely ignoring my own yogurt. "It would never work out anyway. I just think we're too different of people." *There! I said it. Now to explain why it's over and not to offend with my words.* I paused.

"Why?" blurted David before I could collect my next thought. "I thought things were going great between us."

"Yes, they are, but I can't do it."

"You can't do what?"

"I can't be with you."

"This doesn't make any sense. We've been through so much already, and I think we're great together."

"We are great together."

He paused, his brain clicking down possible reasons why I would suddenly break up with him three hours after making out intensely in the back seat of his Suzuki Samurai.

"Was it something my mother said?"

I sighed in relief. It was out in the open. "Yes, it was." At least I could explain myself in honesty instead of having to lie to him. "She said she would make my life a living hell if I got in the way of your calling or whatever." I looked down. A mixture of emotions filled my words, and I couldn't hide them. I didn't want to hide them. "I cannot and do not want to be that person she wants me to be, and I don't want you to have to choose between us. So, it just makes sense to end it now."

"She did what? I thought she was going to talk to you about something totally different."

"That's what she said. A living hell." My eyes teared up.

"For real?"

"I'm not making this up, David. I can't be around your mother."

Understanding and love filled David's face as he realized the real purpose of his mother's "heart-to-heart" with me. We were in love with each other: what she had done to me, she had done to us. Then he spoke.

"If I ever have to choose between you and my mom, I chose you, Trudy." He pushed his yogurt aside and leaned towards me across the table. Then he took my hand in his and said, "I don't want to marry my mother. I want to marry you. I love you."

I put my other hand on his and looked into his eyes, searching. I saw only love.

That was it: Our commitment was sealed, and our choice had been made. It was *us* now, not him and I, but *we*. I took my first bite of yogurt, and it was good. The room didn't feel so cold anymore. I smiled and took a second bite.

CHAPTER IV

IN WHICH
Your Father and Mother Don't Have Sex but do Get Married

4.1

Though we had managed to work through some of our relationship's more difficult parts, we still had the greatest challenge ahead of us: Sex. Or, to be more precise, not having sex. At that time in our lives, David and I believed that a few things could keep a person from getting into heaven. After the Unpardonable Sin, which no one seems to know exactly what it is, there was one other sure-fire, go-to-hell-quickly sin. And that was having sex before marriage, or, in Biblical terms, fornication.

4.2

My Beloved,

I know I should be going to sleep, but I miss you. I have fallen so far in love. I could never have dreamed of this. I have gone far beyond the comfort zone. I think I went beyond that while we were still just friends. Even then, we talked of marriage. I'm telling you I didn't want this to happen. I know you didn't either. I love you holding me and drifting off into another world. I'm scared, yet I can't stop it either.

Something else that scares me is my overwhelming desire to give you all of me. I have never desired that before. This is all new to me. Please be patient. To love and please you is my greatest desire. That is what would make me so very happy. That is why I feel so self-conscious physically. And yet you accept me. I don't get it. It's just a bit overwhelming. I just needed to get this all down.

Trudy

4.3

"You need to wait until you're out of college before you marry him," my mother told me one day as I tried to ignore her. Western Washington's early spring rains, following its continual fall and winter rains, had turned the woods outside our unfinished home into riots of greens that fanned from chartreuse to emerald.

"You need to have your degree."

Funny, the one thing that she continued to tell me I wasn't good enough to accomplish was her fixation. It was almost like the thought of me trying for a degree and failing just like she had amused her and simply was something she had to see for herself.

I poked at an opened can of Fri-Chik. *Yeah, sure.* I thought. *There's no way I'll live that long. I'll die of sexual frustration.*

"Did you hear me, Trudy?" she quizzed.

"Yes," I sighed. "I heard you."

"You don't want your life to turn out like mine," she continued to push. "I didn't get my degree, and now I can't leave Lester, even if I wanted to."

"Mmhmm," I grunted. She assumed my love for David was like hers towards my father? We both knew that wasn't true; when she saw David and me together, she oozed envy. I was confused. Did she want me to get a degree and do well, or did she wish that my life would end up miserable and unfulfilled just like hers? *Either way, she wins,* I thought. *If I succeed, she'll live off my success like a vampire, making it all about her. If I fail, she'll smugly say, "I told you so," with all the satisfaction of a sadist.* I kept my thoughts to myself. Telling her anything only came back to haunt me.

I started adding mayonnaise to the Fri-Chik to make a soy chicken salad sandwich. It was another make-it-yourself dinner that I had become all too familiar with since grade school. In a couple of hours, my father would come home and help himself to half a cantaloupe filled with ice cream for dinner, while my mom would graze her way through the cupboards and fridge for the evening. My sister was the lucky one; she worked swing shift and was already gone.

"I don't know how you'll do it, though," she continued. "Look at how weak you are, Trudy. You're not strong enough to go to school. I know you, and you can't handle it." I guess she had made up her mind on her pitch. I found it amusing that I was already in college full-time and did, in fact, have a

111

part-time job working in a daycare after school. But I thought better of mentioning that to her.

"We're going to wait until David gets his degree before getting married. Then he'll get a job while I finish my degree." Then I turned to face her. "But you already knew that. Nothing has changed."

My words were direct, maybe too blunt, but she knew better than to call me on them. I was in a mood that could match any disapproval she could throw at me—I was so sexually frustrated that no reproach could put a tap on that kind of energy. I slapped the other slice of bread on my fake chicken sandwich so I could escape to my room.

My mom didn't force the issue. She got what she wanted—me at home a little longer to play mind games with. I was in hell with no probation in sight.

4.4

Around the dinner table one evening, David's father, after finishing his T-bone steak, wiped his mouth, then his forehead, with his napkin and placed it under the edge of the plate.

"You know, Tiger," he began, leaning back in his chair and resting his hands on his large, thinning head. "I know you and Trudy are serious, but there are financial considerations that you have to make when you get married." Lilith, sitting across from him, her steak half-eaten, nodded. "Tell me," he leaned forward, resting his arms on the table. "How will you provide for her?"

"I'll get a second job," David said. "Between the two of us, we'll make it."

"That's not a stable life that you're offering her."

"You really should consider this issue, David," Lillith added. "You need to have a degree and consistent income before you get married."

"You shouldn't marry Trudy until you've graduated from college," Adam said. "Because once you get married, you're on your own. I won't help you with your tuition."

And that was the final word.

4.5

Dearest,

I'm so worried about us. I feel as if we're never going to be together. We're going to have to postpone and keep on forever. And I don't want to die before I can be with you. My heart aches for you, for us. I'd love to hear you promise me that everything will be okay. I need to hear that from you now. I just want you. I want to cling to you and never have to let go. I'm being very honest with you. I can't hold out forever. David, I don't even know if I can trust myself with you for that long.

Please don't leave me, David. Oh, my, now I'm crying, and everything is all blurry. I'm such a mess. I love you, David. I need you. This must be awful for you to have to read. I'm sorry. I'll go now.

I am ever yours.

4.6

David, hopelessly in love and equally horny, took to studying and, within a month, had figured out a way to get his Bachelor's Degree in two years. It involved a complicated formula of placement tests, summer classes, and taking twenty credits each semester. But, it was worth it in his mind, so long as we could get married and have sex sooner. It also meant that instead of heading off to an Adventist university, I would spend two years at community college, get my AA, and then transfer to a university. Unfortunately, it also meant that I would have to live another two years at home, a place that I desperately wanted to escape.

4.7

In the fall of 1995, David headed three hundred miles across the state to Spokane for his first year of college. Little changed in our relationship, except that our phone bills got longer, largely in part to the fact that we could never get off the phone.

"You hang up this time," David would say. "I did last time."

Heartsick and longing for his voice, I reluctantly agreed. "I love you," I said.

"I love you, too," David replied.

A long silence filled the air.

"Goodbye," I said.

"Goodbye."

More silence. Then a voice. "Did you hang up?"

"No, I'm still here," I replied. "I couldn't do it."

"Now we have to do it all over again!"

"I know," I sighed. "I love you."

"I love you, too, Trudy. So much."

But it wasn't all bad. Every other week David and I alternated who would make the trip across the state. This weekend David made the drive through the scablands, across the Columbia River, then over Snoqualmie Pass and down to Puget Sound, finally turning on my dirt road and pulling into the driveway of the still-unfinished house. We spent the evening on the sofa in the basement, the fire cranked up, listening to Jim Brickman CDs and whispering sweet nothings to each other. We had to whisper because even though everyone else had gone to bed, my mom had decided to pass out in the recliner, her favorite sleeping spot. While she snored, David wooed me as quietly as possible.

"What's that?" She'd snort herself awake in the middle of our talking before drifting back off. "You're scheming," she mumbled, half asleep. "I can hear you scheming." Then she'd shift her bulk around, the chair squeaking for a moment or two before she dozed again.

Once she had settled, David whispered in my ear, his lips just brushing my hair. "You know, we are scheming, Sunshine."

I smiled. Earlier in the day, David and I headed to the mall, where he picked out a thin gold band for me.

"I can't marry you now, Trudy," he kept whispering, his soft voice gently lulling me. "But this ring is a promise that when we can, I'll marry you."

He slipped the ring on my finger. It shimmered gold in the candlelight.

4.8

My David,

Close your eyes and look deep into mine. There you can find me. There I will give you peace, rest, love, encouragement, and all of my commitment. Through my eyes, you can see yourself the pure way that God has shown me. Look deep, David; it's all there and only for you. I could never love anyone like you. You're my everything, from my handsome prince in shining armor to my best friend and confidant.

4.9

Hello again, Beautiful,

Right now, I am sitting in the dorm lounge by myself, listening to John Denver on the eight-track player I got at a garage sale. John Denver really makes me think of you. I want just to have you in my arms right now and not worry about time. I wish that you could just live under my bed or something. That would be nice. I won't tell anyone if you do. I am committed to you, Trudy Pflugrad, and you alone. Nobody here compares to you in beauty or heart. You are the one I love and no one else. I promise to love you with all my heart. I will come over the horizon for you someday and take you to be my wife.
    Until then, I am ever and always
        Yours

4.10

My Pooky,

I can't stop thinking about us. I want very much to marry you. The feeling is overwhelming. Do you think we will? I do pray so. I hope it's not wrong, but I love you so much I can't even find a reason to study without you near. You are my reason for everything.

You're my missing link—I need you with all my heart. I feel like I have a brain disorder. Something has gone all haywire in my head, and I can't get it back together the way it should. All I know is you. Everything else is a blur.

We can't get married this summer! My hair won't grow out in time! Oh, my, what will I look like? Oh heavens, the things I come up with. You know, the good thing about getting married is that our phone bill would go down, that's for sure.

4.11

Dearest,

I get to see you tomorrow, and I can hardly wait. My whole body is aching for you. I miss you more than I have ever done before. I continually have to fight off daydreams. I wish they were real. I want to marry you, Trudy, and I wish that I could today. I long for you so much.

Each time I see a married couple, I think of you and hope that someday we can share that union. I only desire you, my Sunshine. I want to hold you close to me, to put my face next to yours, to feel the joy of being near to you. I long to run my fingers down your cheek, feeling the softness of your skin. I wish that it were true. We could kiss and lose all sense of reality, enveloped in one another's love.

4.12

David,

I didn't call you because it's not an emergency, and I don't want to cause you stress. But I am so scared. How will we make it? No, I'm not overreacting. I already did that, and I'm glad I didn't call you. I want to marry you, and I want to be happy, also. I'm afraid that I'm going to give up school for our marriage. Then I'll be like my mom, and I can't do that. But I want us to be happy. I'm scared and confused. Do you feel like this, too? Are we going to make it? How can we know? It's a leap of faith. All I know is that I love you, and I'm afraid of losing you.

4.13

Four months later, things were no better. The promise ring had only made it worse. Now that we were committed, each day that we weren't married felt like torture. Once filled with sweet nothings and daydreams, our letters to each other had changed to factual details about our classes, friends, and life events. "It's too much, Trudy," David told me. "I can't handle reading your letters. I'm going to have to be cold if we're going to make it two more years and not have sex."

It felt like those two years were two too many. Even trying to count down each day taunted and tormented us. So it was one cold February evening just north of Spokane, Washington. Several feet of snow blanketed the yard of my aunt's house, where I stayed while visiting David. Christmas lights, still buried in snow, wouldn't likely be put away until the thaw in March or April. It was in the teens that clear night, but the home felt snug and warm inside. The red glow of the pellet stove lit the room, while just outside the large windows, stars glittered brightly in the winter sky. It was cozy inside, and David put off the drive back to his dorm room as long as he could.

"How are we going to make it another year and four months, Trudy?" David asked me earnestly.

"I don't know." I stared out the window. It felt hopeless.

"I'm serious," he turned towards me, forcing me to break my trance and give him all of my attention. His eyes searched mine.

"I'm serious, too," I interjected, letting him know I felt just as hopeless.

David leaned back against the sofa in desperation. What could we do? It wasn't that family didn't have our best interests in mind. David was only nineteen, and his health was far from optimal. He'd already had numerous surgeries, and as my physical therapist dad so bluntly put it, was realistically only two years from being in a wheelchair. I knew the road I had chosen wasn't going to be an easy one. I was marrying a cripple with no hope of him getting better; there is still no cure for arthritis. But I had fallen in love with David and didn't want to marry anyone I didn't love.

Doesn't love conquer all in the end? Well, my parents didn't think so. And I knew I did not have their approval to marry David, even if he converted to Seventh-day Adventism. They thought reason would come to my stubborn mind before it was too late. Meanwhile, David's parents were happy that David landed a caretaker: I wanted to be a nurse. What luck for David! Either way, we were young, far too young.

"I've got it!" David interjected, stopping my wandering mind. "Why don't we elope? Then we can have sex and still go to school. We'll just see each other every weekend."

"Elope?" I yelped. "How could we keep that a secret? Besides, once we're married, I'd want to live with you, not sneak away on weekends."

He knew I was right and didn't try to argue my point. But more than anything, for better or worse, we wanted to be together. The separation had become unbearable.

"I just don't see how we are going to hold out another year, Trudy," David sighed. "Then what?" The *what* part of that sentence bothered me. We would never forgive ourselves or each other if we had sex before marriage. It was unimaginable and as good as going to hell. Who knows? Maybe hell would be better, but we didn't want to find out. Silence settled back into the cozy home as the stove fan hummed in the background.

Then David, filled with sudden determination, slipped his hand over mine, gave it a gentle squeeze, and stiffly slid off the couch to one knee.

"Oh, no, you don't!" I exclaimed, terrified of what was about to happen. David grinned a cheesy romantic grin and playfully batted his eyelashes, a coy look in his eyes. I pulled on his arms, trying to get him back onto the sofa, but he was resolved, stubborn, and solid as a pillar of stone.

"Trudy Pflugrad," he paused for dramatic effect. "Will you marry me?"

"We can't, and you know that!" I countered.

"I know. Will you marry me?"

"Stop it, David!" I argued, protested, and sputtered, but the pillar wouldn't budge. He wasn't going to get off the floor until I gave him an answer.

Finally, in exasperation, I replied, "I don't know. I have to think about it." Then I left him on the floor and headed downstairs to the basement for a moment to think. *Caution has always been my chief ally*, I thought, using all my reasoning skills. *Rushing a marriage does not make financial or educational sense. Plus, our parents want us to wait another year.*

But I love him with all my heart and want to be with him forever, my emotions countered. *And if we don't get married soon, I'll either have sex with him and go to hell or die from frustration.*

Both sides had valid points, but in the end, my emotions won. I made my way back up the stairs while David kneeled, waiting for my reply.

"Yes! I will marry you," I said, sitting down on the couch. A sense of relief and salvation filled the room as David finally raised himself off the floor and embraced me, not as my boyfriend but as my fiancé. "But I would like an engagement ring," I laughed.

4.14

My Dearest,

We're going to make it, David. Everything is going to work out. Once we're formally engaged with the ring and all, time will fly by. It will be the big countdown. I'm so excited! I want to be tied down. That sounds awful, I know. With all of my heart, I love you and am committed to you and us. I'm going to be the best wife that I can be. I promise you that.

You know, we're going to have to budget chocolate in somewhere when we marry. I get these uncontrollable cravings for it just before D-Day. It's not a pretty sight if I don't get it. I just thought I'd give you forewarning.

David, I am radiating happiness. My joy is overflowing. My heart and my soul are leaping from within. I am yours, David. I am patiently waiting for my groom. All my dreams are coming true.

4.15

My Only Sunshine,

I didn't think that getting engaged would make things so much harder. I thought it would help. The scary thought is that it will only get worse. My daydreams are horrible. I am so ready to spend my life with you. I need you, Trudy Pflugrad. July 14th seems so far away. I miss having you near. I want to call you Mrs. Trudy Wakefield, my wife. I love you, dearest, and I am longing for you. Oh, marriage is so far away! I don't know if I will make it. Yes, I will, but 4 ½ months! (Four months, two weeks, and one day, to be exact). All that I can think about, dream about, is you. I love you. I promise to take good care of you, my Sunshine. I am in this for better or worse.

4.16

It was only minutes from the start of the ceremony. The muted hum of the organ softly echoed as I watched guests making their way down the aisle to find their seats. The darkness of the mother's room just off the side of the sanctuary kept me hidden as I looked through the one-way glass at people's happy faces greeting each other with whispers and smiles. The chatter and bustle of last-minute preparations were now far out of my reach, and I could only look on until the big moment.

My father stood near the door of the room, awaiting the signal for our departure. Nervous, giddy thoughts flitted through my mind in anticipation of one of life's greatest events. I felt both happy and guilty to be sharing it with my dad. I was leaving him, the only person before David who had even pretended to believe in me.

How sad that is, now that I think about it.

"You know, Trudy. It's not too late." His words split through the soft silence. Suddenly the organ and happy faces disappeared, and I was all alone. I couldn't decide if it was nerves I felt or if I was just now hearing something I should have thought of before this moment. My heart skipped a beat. My mind swam.

"Are you sure you want to do this?" His voice swooned through the room. "He's going to be in a wheelchair by the time he's thirty."

Suddenly I wasn't sure. My dad did know what he was talking about. He specialized in these kinds of cases and had years of experience seeing what arthritis could do to a person. His observations of David's progression and poor response to the massive amounts of medications he had to take made my dad's timeline entirely rational.

Not only that, but until he yelled at me about David, my father could do no wrong in my life, despite his angry tirades. Being in a family where alliances and favoritism were the norms, I cast my vote at a very young age in my father's favor. In return, I received his years of advice and protection against my mother, who resented me from the day she knew I existed. It wasn't like my father was smart by everyday standards, but his wisdom and advice on people always proved sound and strangely spot-on. He could read people and interactions like a book. And he probably was right about David.

I panicked. *What am I doing? Am I making the biggest mistake of my life?* For the first time in my relationship with David, I saw that my life would be hard, very hard if I married him. *How have I not thought this through before?* It was as if someone had taken off my rose-colored glasses for the first time, and I could truly see. *How foolish of me to just now realize all of this*, I thought. *And on my wedding day!*

"It's not too late at all." My father's words drew closer as he left the door and walked to my side. "I could call it off for you right now." He stood next to me as a support. It all became perfectly clear to me. *This isn't the life I really wanted, is it?* My heart was breaking, and I felt it. There was no one I wanted to disappoint more in my life than my father. I lived for his approval, and now I had lost it. I had always known he disapproved of David, but he'd been silent about my relationship with him since our last fallout. He had saved his true heart until this moment, forcing me to choose between him and the man I loved. *How can I choose?* I thought. *His logic makes sense, while David's been a foolish whim.*

Was it a whim? I rightly didn't know. My mind filled with confusion; it seemed the room was spinning. I could see David waiting for me at the altar, standing awkwardly in his tuxedo. Meanwhile, my dad stood next to me, waiting for my response. *But what will I say?*

Out of nowhere, I heard words from somewhere in my head, clear as a fresh breeze cutting through smoke. "I will heal him," the voice said. "It will be okay." My mind grew clear, and peace filled me once again. I couldn't explain what had just happened, but it was as real as my father's voice standing next to me. I saw the beginning of a new road ahead and knew I could walk it. I knew that I would be okay.

The words spoke so clear, so loud in my mind, like a promise for me. I breathed out deeply—I must have been holding my breath for quite some time. My resolve formed first in my mind. Suddenly I found my feet and knew where I was, waiting to marry the man I loved. The organ continued its happy, muted tune. Once again, the people and smiling faces stood in front of me, just on the other side of the glass.

I breathed a new fresh breath, my own. The road hadn't changed. I knew it would be hard, but I would be alright. I would break my father's heart.

"No. I want to marry David," I said.

He slunk away. "Okay," came his defeated response. My father shrunk into silence, resuming his previous spot by the door. I once again breathed deeply in my promise, my hope, and my salvation into my full stature.

The door quietly opened. It was time. My father paused, making sure of my resolve as I walked out of the dim room, past him, and through the doorway. I turned down the hallway, feeling the carpeted floor through my shoes. The July sunlight glowed through the windows of the foyer, untinted or dulled by the glass. I blinked, welcoming in its rays as my eyes adjusted back into daylight.

My nerves returned, but this time it was because of excitement and anticipation. I breathed out a deep, shaky, hopeful breath ever so slowly, then turned towards the sanctuary, the sun glowing against my back. My father came to my side.

"I'll walk as fast or slow as you," he said. "You set the pace." I nodded that I understood. I take the lead.

The organ trumpeted with all its might. A helping hand straightened out my train, and it billowed behind me, full and beautiful. The congregation rose and turned in anticipation; every eye focused on me.

I took my father's arm, following a trail of rose petals laying on the long white carpet that bridged the gap between David and me.

My footsteps filled the gap.

Is it appropriate to say, out of the frying pan and into the fire here, kids?

No?

Okay. I won't say it, then.

The All New God, Sex and Money Diet

Made in the USA
Columbia, SC
28 June 2023